The Dogrib Indians are one of the Dene groups—Athapaskan-speaking peoples of the western Canadian Subarctic. Based on the author's field studies from 1959 to 1976, this volume presents an ethnographic description of the Dogrib prophet movement. Part 1 introduces three prophets who came to prominence in the 1960s and 1970s. Although they developed from the same cultural background and had the same aims, their prophetic styles contrasted dramatically with one another. Helm situates the prophet movement in relation to both aboriginal and Christian traditions and shows the determining importance of the prophets' personalities in shaping their practice of prophecy.

Part 2 examines the traditional Dogrib concept of power *(ink'on)*, which underlies the prophet movement. It draws together information given over the course of years by Vital Thomas, a Dogrib who collaborated closely with Helm. This first-hand material is noteworthy for its personal perspective and for the understanding it provides of the differing sources and uses of power. The concept of power is so pervasive in daily life that it forms the key for understanding the dynamics of Dogrib culture. The book concludes with a brief autobiography related by Vital Thomas.

JUNE HELM received a Ph.D. from the University of Chicago and has for many years been a professor of anthropology at the University of Iowa. She is the editor of *Subarctic,* volume 6 of the *Handbook of North American Indians,* published by the Smithsonian Institution (1981).

STUDIES
IN THE ANTHROPOLOGY OF
NORTH AMERICAN INDIANS

Editors
Raymond J. DeMallie
Douglas R. Parks

PROPHECY AND POWER
AMONG
THE DOGRIB INDIANS
June Helm

Published by the University of Nebraska Press
Lincoln and London

In cooperation with the American Indian Studies Research
Institute, Indiana University, Bloomington

© 1994 by the University of Nebraska Press
Manufactured in the United States of America
The paper in this book meets the minimum requirements
of American National Standard for Information Sciences—
Permanence of Paper for Printed Library Materials, ANSI Z39.48-1984.
Library of Congress Cataloging-in-Publication Data
Helm, June, 1924–
Prophecy and power among the Dogrib Indians / June Helm.
        p.   cm. – (Studies in the anthropology of North American
Indians) "In cooperation with the American Indian Studies Research
Institute, Indiana University, Bloomington."
Includes bibliographical references (p.   ) and index.
ISBN 0-8032-2373-0 (cloth: acid-free paper)
1. Thlingchadinne Indians – Religion.
2. Thlingchadinne mythology.   3. Nativistic movements –
Northwest Territories.   4. Shamanism – Northwest
Territories.   5. Thlingchadinne Indians – Folklore.
I. Indiana University. American Indian Studies Research
Institute.   II. Title.   III. Series.
E99.T4H45   1994   299'.782 – dc20
94-11841   CIP

To the Memory of

Vital Thomas

Contents

PART TWO

INK'ON

Illustrations

Preface and Acknowledgments

I began to develop "Three Styles in the Practice of Prophecy" (part 1 of this volume) in 1986, but other scholarly enterprises and extraneous impediments intervened to prevent the next-to-final reworking of the draft manuscript until 1991. Only then did it occur to me that the addition of *Ink'on* (part 2) would by illustration buttress the summary assertions about Dogrib medicine power in my study of Dogrib prophecy. Even more, I came to realize that if I did not now make the effort to treat in some form the accounts of medicine power in my field notes, the data would most likely disappear. The two parts of this volume, then, are written in different styles and from different angles and with different intentions. Each part is relatively self-contained. But taken together they allow, I hope, an appreciation of Dogrib cultural style.

Nancy Oestreich Lurie and I worked together in three field seasons (1959, 1962, 1967) among the Dogribs and always shared the compiling of field notes as well as the pleasures and pains of fieldwork. Beryl C. Gillespie has shared her notes on the prophet movement from the perspective of the Dogrib community of Dettah. Robert Howren, who was with me coinvestigator under a National Science Foundation Research Grant (1970–74), provided not only linguistic data—his own speciality—but also information on the activities of prophets at Rae. Under the NSF grant, Virginia Lawson, George Tharp, and Stanley Witkowski as linguistic field researchers among the Beaver, Slavey, and Bearlake Dene gleaned information about prophet activities and interests of those peoples. Early in the drafting of the prophet study, Jean-Guy Goulet and Earl Waugh provided information on the Alberta prophet movement and the ecumenical activities at Ste. Anne, respectively. Scott Rushforth and David M. Smith have stimulated my thinking about *ink'on* from their respective research vantage points of Fort Franklin and Fort Resolution. The National Museum of Canada and the University of Iowa supported several of my visits to the Dogribs.

Beyond my profound debt to Vital Thomas, I am beholden to the many Dogribs who proffered help, friendship, and the example of the conduct of their lives. I hope they realized how grateful I have been for their kindnesses and how much I have enjoyed their friendships. I think expecially of Susie (Joseph) Abel, Johnny Base, Harry Bearlake, Elise Beaulieu, Therese Beaulieu, Jimmie Bruneau, Susie (Joseph) Bruneau, Alexis Charlo, Alexis Crapeau, Jimmy Drybones, Joe Drybones, Rosalie Drybones, Laiza Dryneck, Jim Erasmus, Alphonse Eronchi, Jim Fish, Alexis Flanki, Jonas Jeremikc'a, Mary Adele Jeremikc'a, Elizabeth Mackenzie, Roseanna Mackenzie, Bruno Moosenose, Joseph Naidzo (Naedzo), Alexis Nitsiza, Elise Nitsiza, Adele Pig, Firmin Pomi, Andrew Ts'etta, Roseanna Ts'etta, James Wah-Shee, Monique Wanazah, Cecile Wetade, and Isadore (Fish) Zoe.

Orthography

The few Dogrib words in the text are rendered in the workaday orthography, not consistently phonemic or phonetic, of my ethnographic field notes. The only symbols that do not have an approximately comparable sound or usage in English are:

c   as in English *chip*.

n   indicates nasalization of the vowel(s) that immediately precede it, as in French *chanson;* n between vowels is sounded as a consonant, as in Dogrib *inin* 'spirit'.

š   as in English *ship*.

x   as in Spanish *jarro*.

z   as in French *azure*.

'   indicates glottalization of the preceding consonant or consonant cluster.

Tone is not indicated, nor is word-initial glottal stop.

Introduction

North American Indian prophets and prophet movements have long attracted the attention of anthropologists. They have inspired a substantial body of analysis and theory on nativistic, messianic (embracing millenarian) and revitalistic movements, as well as crisis cults. On New Year's day 1892, James Mooney (1896) interviewed the Paiute prophet Wovoka. For twenty-two months before and after that interview Mooney pursued in the field the reactions of tribesmen throughout the American West to Wovoka's message of the Ghost Dance. From that time on, most ethnologists seeking evidence on the character and persona of Native American prophets have had to rely on the fading memories of native persons relaying their own observations or the accounts they gained from prior generations, or, especially in those cases far back in time, only the reports and assessments of Euro-American observers. Several modern investigators, however, have had the opportunity to evoke recent memory of dead prophets and see prophets in action among Dene peoples—Athapaskan-speaking Indians—of northwestern Canada. Materials recently have been published on prophecy among the Beaver and Slavey Dene of British Columbia and Alberta (and will be fleetingly referred to in this study). The interests of those investigators, however, are very distinct from those I bring to this study of prophets among the Dogrib Dene.

I started ethnographic field research among the Northern Dene in 1952 in a small Slavey settlement on the bank of the Mackenzie River in the Northwest Territories of Canada. In 1959 I began work among the Dogribs of Lac la Martre, shifting in 1962 to Rae, the Dogrib "capital." By then change was proceeding apace in the lives, circumstances, and experiences of the Dogrib people (Helm 1979, 1980). From 1967 to 1976 I returned to Rae for two or three weeks almost every year. To track social and political developments I usually arrived at "treaty time" (of which, more in the text), when issues between the government and the Indians surfaced. In the process of keeping up with events I began to hear about the contact of some Dogribs with Dene prophets to the south, in northern Alberta, and then to learn that the Dogribs now had their own prophets. So, as has generally been the case, data emerging in the field turned me to attend to a subject I had not contemplated before.

Prophecy is "the work, function, or vocation of a prophet," and the prophecies of the three protagonists of this study conform nicely to the dictionary characterization: *"Jewish & Christian Theol[ogy],* inspired declaration or revelation of the divine word, including moral teaching by warning, consoling, exhorting, giving an example of fellowship with God, and the like" *(Webster's New International Dictionary,* 1940). These Dogrib prophecies, however, did not include the particular characteristic that the dictionary goes on to describe as "on special occasions . . . of foretelling, of declaring beforehand, the purpose of God."

The emphasis in this study is not on "culture" nor is the subject "religion," although the activities of the prophets and the attention of the Dogrib people were certainly on topics that are usually subsumed under those rubrics. The focus, as indicated in the title, is on the public careers of three Dogrib prophets who emerged in the late 1960s and on the distinctive character and personal style that each brought to his role.

This inquiry in part treats of the opinions that individual Dogribs held of each of the Dogrib prophets and of the prophets' opinions of each other. Their expressions of unfavorable judgments, kinds of opposition, and dislikes call for sensitivity on my part to what I believe might be the wishes of certain persons respecting anonymity. Also, old-time manners require that persons' names not be mentioned casually. Therefore, with two exceptions, the names of persons living at the time of the fieldwork among the Dogribs have been altered. I have assigned pseudonyms to two of the prophets; I call them Jack the Rae Prophet and Chi the Marten Lake Prophet. However, I use the Bear Lake Prophet's actual name, Naidzo. Naidzo's evident gratification with his fame among Dene and sympathetic whites as a significant and respected figure led me in this and other writings to accord him the overt recognition I am confident he would have desired.

Part 2, *"Ink'on,"* presents the lore and knowledge about medicine power that my long-time Dogrib friend and consultant Vital Thomas provided through the years as my steno pads filled on all kinds of topics. His acerbic opinion of one prophet led me to assign Vital a pseudonym in the writing of "Three Styles." Then in 1990 Vital Thomas died. Given his departure and my certain knowledge that he so much enjoyed recognition for his command of the history and lore of the Dogrib people,

I have decided to continue to make clear in part 1, as I have elsewhere, the significance of Vital Thomas' contribution to the record of Dogrib culture and history.

PART ONE

Three Styles in the Practice of

Prophecy

1

Prelude to Prophecy

To Set the Stage

The Dogribs are one of the Dene peoples, Athapaskan-speaking Indians, who inhabit the western subarctic of North America. (For ethnographic and ethnohistorical summaries on the Dogribs, see Helm 1972, 1981a). The Dogrib range comprises that portion of the rocky upland Canadian Shield and bordering plain that drain into the North Arm of Great Slave Lake in the District of Mackenzie of Canada's Northwest Territories. Hunting caribou and moose, snaring hare, fishing, and, after "contact," trapping fur animals, Dogribs lived off the bush, an open coniferous woodland interspersed with thousands of lakes. For several decades before this study, official Canadian government "band rolls" had segregated the Dogrib collectivity into two administrative sets, Yellowknife B Band and Dog Rib Rae Band. The band rolls enumerated all "treaty Indians," descendants of persons officially recognized as Indians under two treaties. Dogribs who traded into Fort Resolution on the south side of Great Slave Lake "took Treaty" in 1900 under Treaty No. 8; these became the Yellowknife B Band in the official nomenclature. The remainder, and greater number of the Dogribs, took Treaty in 1921 under Treaty No. 11; these Dogribs, who traded into Fort Rae, were designated the Dog Rib Rae Band. Each summer at treaty time, a government representative "paid treaty" at the fort—five dollars to each treaty Indian, with councillors receiving fifteen dollars and chiefs twenty-five—and issued ammunition and fishing-net twine to household heads, directly or through the councillors or chief. (See appendix for descriptions of these statuses.) The treaty payments encouraged even more a seasonal congregation of folk, especially the men, at the fort, where they were already accustomed to gathering after the "spring hunt" to trade their beaver and muskrat pelts and enjoy group feasts, dances, and games. Also, in the decades following the establishment of the Roman

7

Rae in 1959. Rae is on Marian Lake, which is separated by Frank's Channel from the North Arm of Great Slave Lake. A bridge links Hudson's Bay Island (left), with the Company's compound of buildings, to Priests' Island, with its hospital-church-mission house complex. On the other side of the island a bridge leads to Murphy's Point on the mainland. Big Boiling Mouth, the father of Murphy (Monhwi), built the first cabin of New Fort Rae on the Point. In 1902 he persuaded the "free trader" firm of Hislop and Nagle to move from Old Fort Rae on the North Arm. New Fort Rae emerged in 1906 when the mission, and then the Hudson's Bay Company, followed.

Summer visitors encamped on the precambrian shield on the north end of Hudson's Bay Island. Rae, 1962.

Catholic faith among the Dogribs in the 1860s and 1870s, Christmas and Easter became focal times for ingathering and festivities at the site of the trading post and mission.

The government count of January 1970 assigned 1,202 Dogribs to the Rae jurisdiction and 504 to the Yellowknife B jurisdiction, a total of 1706 (Canada 1970:5, 37). The Yellowknife B Band rolls purportedly specified those Dogribs who resided at Dettah, a small Dogrib settlement across Yellowknife Bay from the city of Yellowknife (which began as a gold-mining camp in the 1930s), and in the Latham Island section of that city. Actually, a number of persons listed on the Yellowknife B roll had for years lived in Rae or the Rae area. On the Rae roll were those "treaty Indians" who lived at the settlement of Rae plus the occupants of several outlying bush hamlets who traded into Rae. With the completion in 1960 of the seventy-mile gravel "highway" between Yellowknife and Rae (and on to Southern Canada) and the inauguration of a twice- or thrice-weekly bus service, Dogribs from Rae and Yellowknife-Dettah were able to see one another frequently.

Before the 1950s, Rae, like the other "forts" in the Mackenzie District, was the site of the trading post, the mission, and within the twentieth century the "mountie" post; Rae also had a small hospital staffed by members of the order of Grey Nuns. For most Dene the fort was a place they visited but where only a very few families (and most of those métis) had log cabin residences. Beginning in the 1950s, the establishment of the Rae day school and a complex of welfare and health services, followed by government-built housing, progressively attracted more and more Dogrib families to live in Rae. The number of resident whites grew (e.g., teachers, a physician, a couple of entrepreneurs and their families). Fort Rae had by then become Rae, a small town that in 1970 was officially incorporated as a hamlet with a governing council apart from the Indian band council.

By 1970 many of the Dogribs in the Rae Band jurisdiction had houses in Rae, which served as single or extended family households. From Rae, men carried out trapping and hunting tours in season. Some families in the Rae jurisdiction continued to live seasonally or year-round in bush settlements within their traditional regional band areas. The main cabin clusters satellite to Rae were at Lac la Martre, in the Marten Lake regional band, *tsontigot'in*/Filth Lake People area; at Snare Lake, in the Edge-of-the-Woods People/*detcinlahot'in* area; and at Marian River Village and Rae Lakes, in the *et'at'in* band/People-Next-to-Another-People area. The hunting-trapping range of the *et'at'in* sometimes extended north over the height-of-land into the Great Bear Lake drainage.

Dogrib country of precambrian rock and boreal forest, part of the range of the *et'at'in* regional band. 1976.

In addition to the people enumerated on the official band rolls of Rae and Yellowknife B, Dene Indians of Dogrib antecedents lived in or traded into the settlement of Fort Franklin on Great Bear Lake. Their range abutted that of the *et'at'in.* For the Rae and, especially, Yellowknife B Dogribs, contacts with this group, the Bear Lake Dogribs, had been tenuous since that band ceased to trade into Rae after 1914.[1] It was in fact the rise of the Dogrib prophet activities that brought a flurry of communication between the main Dogrib body of the Great Slave Lake drainage and the Fort Franklin people.

Between 1967 and 1971, all people of native heritage within the Rae-Yellowknife interaction sphere composed a cognized society. All reasonably knowledgeable adult natives knew or knew of one another and one another's family lines. Within this kith-and-kin collectivity there was a minority of adults who, by family background or through schooling combined with special employment opportunities, had had greater experience and involvement with the Euro-Canadian system. Such persons were effectively bilingual in Dogrib and English. This category comprised certain individual adult Dogribs plus those several families recognized by themselves and the rest of the community to have a distinctive native identity as "halfbreeds" or métis (see Slobodin 1981).

Almost all métis families at Rae, most of whom bear the same surname, were officially Dogrib "Indians," recognized by the government as descendants of persons of native heritage who took Treaty in 1921. By far the great majority of Dogrib families were bush Indians, oriented to taking caribou, moose, hare, and fish for subsistence, and fur bearers for income. The adults were predominantly monolingual in Dogrib. By 1970, however, the generation gap between mature Dogribs and their children was on its way to becoming a culture gap, as J. G. E. Smith (1978) observed in another Dene society of the 1970s. Parents' life experiences stood in contrast to those of their immature and some of their young adult offspring, who since the 1950s had gone through a few years of white man's schooling, had at least a basic command of English, and were involved with aspects of modern Euro-Canadian culture, especially youth culture. By 1970 a handful of young Dogribs who had undertaken secondary or postsecondary schooling at points south had returned home; three of the young men, especially, were committed Indian rights activists.

Of the approximately 1700 Dogribs in the Rae-Yellowknife interaction sphere, it was the adults who composed the significant audience for the Dogrib prophets. From the Rae and Yellowknife B band rolls issued 31 December 1970, I have segregated adults from juveniles. For present purposes *adult* is defined as all husband-wife pairs in which the husband was twenty or older (born in or before 1950), as well as widowed or single persons twenty or older as of 1970. Table 1 presents a breakdown of adults by marital status and age group. Altogether, they add up to 767 individuals. By Dogrib evaluations, my definition of *adult* is very generous. For example, an unmarried man in his twenties (there were 75 in the study) is hardly regarded by Dogribs as an adult. But, hewing to the most generous definition, about 770 persons comprised the adult audience, a body of opinion, and potential believers in the authenticity of the Dogrib prophets. Their responses, assessments, and exchanges with one another and the protagonists shaped the course of the Dogrib prophet movement. Differentials in judgmental authority within this body will be assessed later.

The protagonists were the three Dogrib prophets, introduced for the moment only by name: Naidzo the Bear Lake Prophet (b. 1887), Jack the Rae Prophet (b. 1919), and Chi the Marten Lake Prophet (b. 1891). Two persons of great importance in terms of their relationships with the prophets and their position in the community were Barthelemy and the Old Chief. Barthelemy (b. 1890) had for years held the official status of band councillor *(gwatía* 'little chief') for those Dogribs and Dogrib métis

Table 1. Adults Registered on Rae and Yellowknife B Band Rolls as of 31 December 1970

Year born	Marital pair by age of husband	Widows or single persons		Men only	Age
		Men	Women		
before 1891	5	7	10	12	80+
1891–1900	21	10	15	31	79–70
1901–1910	28	6	17	34	69–60
1911–1920	56	6	5	62	59–50
1921–1930	54	20	15	74	49–40
1931–1940	51	21	19	72	39–30
1941–1950	31	75	49	106	29–20
	(246 x 2=)				
T persons	492	145	130	391	

residing wholly at Rae. He was a respected elder, a stern moralist, and a devout Roman Catholic. The Old Chief (b. 1882) was officially the head chief for all Dogribs registered on the Rae band rolls. Not officially connected with the Yellowknife B Band, which had its own chief, the Old Chief nonetheless represented for them as well as for the Rae Dog Ribs an embodiment of the Dogrib as a people. A sixth person must be accorded special mention. Since 1962 Vital Thomas (b. 1904), a Dogrib resident of Rae, had been my interpreter, teacher, friend, landlord, and conduit of communication with older monolingual men. The aversion Vital developed to Jack the Rae Prophet blocked me from investigative interaction with Jack and his monolingual followers.

Several other Dogribs acquired the epithet *prophet* during this period. One was a Dogrib (b. 1915) from Dettah employed at Fort Simpson in the region of the Slavey, a neighboring Dene people. In addition, five or six Rae Dogribs became minor prophets ("minor" is my designation) as followers and cultic assistants to the Rae Prophet. All were middle-aged or older. One woman was said to be a prophet, but she was not in evidence at the prophet ceremony I attended (see below). The minor prophets did not orchestrate prophet dances, as Jack did, or otherwise become public figures and preachers, as did Naidzo, Chi, and Jack. When apart from Jack, their ritual observances (e.g., prophet drumming and singing) were personal or familial and drew no public involvement. These secondary prophets will be treated only in passing.

The prophetic effectuations of Naidzo, Jack, and Chi and the events and activities among the Dogribs that revolved around the three men I shall refer to, generically and loosely, as the Dogrib prophet movement. They compose the manifold text of the Dogrib prophet drama between 1967 and 1971, although the story will occasionally go beyond the latter date.

The Dogrib prophet movement began in travels and communications south into the province of Alberta. For at least two years before 1966, traveling the gravel highway from Yellowknife-Rae to the south, a few Dogribs had made summer pilgrimages to the Roman Catholic camp meeting of Cree and other southern Indians at the holy curative waters of Lac Ste. Anne, west of Edmonton in southern Alberta. In the summer of 1966 Barthelemy, concerned about his wife's ill health, journeyed to join the assemblage at Lac Ste. Anne. At this point the travels and communications directly pertinent to the Dogrib prophet movement began. They are chronologically enumerated below and keyed to Figure 1.

Travels and Contacts in the Dogrib Prophet Movement

1. Summer 1966 Barthelemy and "half a dozen fellows" traveled by highway to Ste. Anne. Apparently learning at Ste. Anne of prophets active among the Slavey of the Hay Lakes-Meander River-Indian Cabins area of northern Alberta,[2] the Dogribs stopped for a weekend while en route back to Rae. The Slavey prophets were carrying out ritual dances. The central figure among them, hereafter referred to as the Alberta Prophet, impressed Barthelemy with his preaching against drink.

2. Christmas 1966 Invited by a letter from (written for) Barthelemy, the Alberta Prophet came by bus to Rae to visit and preach. Some of the Dogrib people from Fort Franklin also arrived in Rae at this time.

3. Easter 1967 The Alberta Prophet again visited Rae by bus.

4. July 1967 Returning from Ste. Anne, a "busload" of Dogribs from Rae—at least eighteen men, including Jack, and their wives—visited the Hay Lakes area and the prophets there for two weeks. (Most of the Dogrib travelers returned by bus to Rae, but some chartered a plane to Fort Simpson in Slavey country on the Mackenzie River to visit the prophet from Dettah who was employed there.) Jack returned to Rae a prophet, bringing with him the Alberta-style ritual. Those who became minor prophets at Rae were also inspired at this time.

5. February-March 1968 By this time the Rae Dogribs had learned of the Bear Lake Prophet, Naidzo. Jack and about thirty people with fifteen dogteams made the overland journey from Rae to Fort Franklin. Besides visiting Naidzo, the purpose of Jack's visit was to "tell people there that he [Jack] is a prophet."

6. *Late summer 1968* A number of Dogribs went by highway from Rae to the Hay Lakes area to visit the Alberta Prophet.

7. *Easter 1969* Easter saw an ingathering of major prophets at Rae. Besides Jack, in residence at Rae, the Alberta Prophet and his wife came by bus for three weeks. Naidzo the Bear Lake Prophet came to Rae by plane, his trip financed by the Rae Dogribs. Several of the minor prophets from Alberta also visited, as did people from outlying Dogrib bush communities as well as some Dene (Slavey and Chipewyan) from farther afield.

8. *July 1969* Jack and other Dogribs visited the Hay Lakes area by bus.

9. *Christmas-New Year 1969-1970* The Bear Lake Prophet again came from Franklin to Rae by plane for a three-week visit. One of the two Catholic priests at Rae radioed the news to outlying Dogrib bush settlements (and, at Vital's request, telegraphed me; I arrived a few days later). The Lac la Martre Indians traveled to Rae by chartered ski-plane. With them was Chi the Marten Lake Prophet. Some Slaveys from the Hay Lakes area and the Chipewyan chief from Snowdrift also came to Rae. The chief from Dettah, the hamlet of the Yellowknife B Dogribs, came to the 29 December feast at Rae, as did the Dettah Prophet, on a visit home from his employment at Fort Simpson.

10. *Easter 1970* There was an exchange of visits between some of the Hay Lakes Alberta Dene and Jack and some Rae Dogribs.

11. *July-August 1970* Jack and three or four of his minor prophet followers proceeded down the Mackenzie River from Fort Providence in two canoes. (A highway freighting company in Yellowknife was contracted to transport the canoes by truck from Rae to Fort Providence.) Jack and his entourage visited forts Simpson, Wrigley, and Norman (Slavey trading post settlements), Fort Franklin (trading post settlement of the Bearlake Dene), and Fort Good Hope (trading-post settlement of the Hare division of the Dene) and returned up the Mackenzie by canoe.

12. *Easter 1971* The Bear Lake Prophet went by plane from Franklin to Rae; he also visited Dettah. By then another mode of communication was operating. A month earlier, the Dettah Prophet received two cassette recordings from Naidzo, who sent another cassette at Christmastime.

After this time, documentation on travels is incomplete. In August 1972 a busload of Dogribs traveled from Rae to Morley, the Stoney Indian reserve in southern Alberta, to attend an ecumenical meeting on

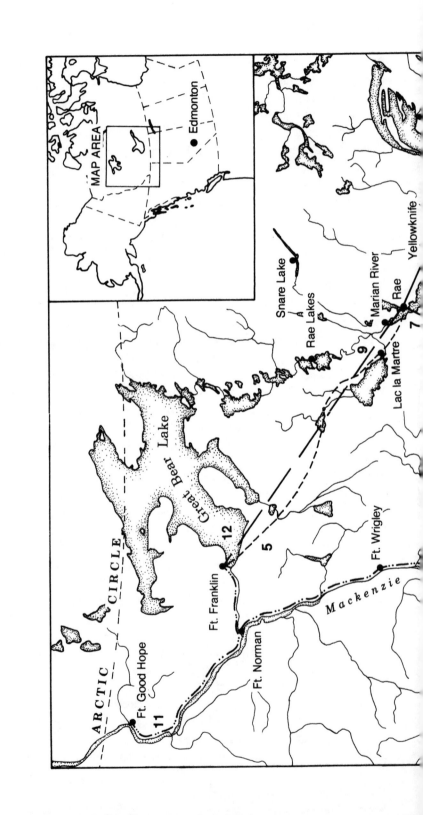

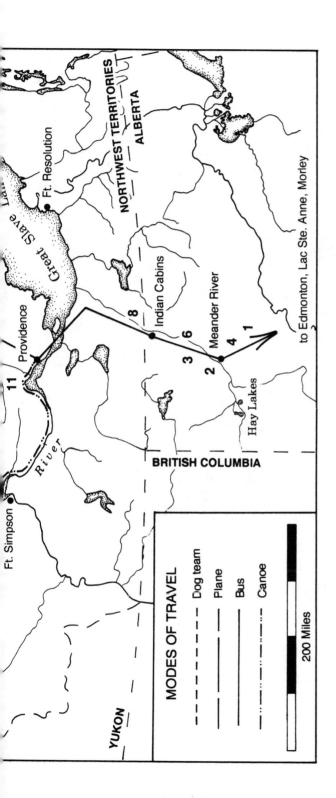

Figure 1. Major Travels and Contacts in the Dogrib Prophet Movement, 1966–71. The travels numbered 1 through 12 are discussed in the text. To give a sense of scale of travels, the river-route distance between Providence and Fort Good Hope (11 to 11) is approximately 640 miles.

Canoe alongside the bridge across the "sny" *(chenal)* between Priests' Island and Hudson's Bay Island, with the Hudson's Bay Company's buildings in the background. Rae, 1962.

Indian religion and medicine power. (For an account of this ecumenical movement, see Stanley 1977). In 1973 Jack visited the Alberta Prophet and planned another summer canoe trip down the Mackenzie River "to see everyone" again. Receiving word that Naidzo had taken ill, Rae Dogribs visited the Bear Lake Prophet shortly before he died at Fort Franklin early in 1973.[3]

* * *

This study is not about causalities—what caused the Dogrib prophet movement and even less what caused Naidzo, Jack, and Chi to assume prophecy, except by their own report. Rather, it is about prophetic presentations and people's responses. The status of *nate,* rendered as 'dreamer' or 'prophet' in English, has traditionally existed within the Dogrib cultural repertoire as a potentially mobilizable role. It is for the prophet's audience to decide, severally and collectively, if the prophet is true—that is, that his prophetic experiences are real and that his message has import for their own lives and values. It was in this context that Barthelemy and other Dogribs sought out and responded to the Alberta prophets. Those first contacts with the Slavey prophets and the visit of the Alberta Prophet to Rae, the heart of Dogrib society, at Christmas 1966 surely helped to prepare the stage for the attention, excitement, and hope that the three Dogrib prophets evoked. It seems clear, however, that only Jack and the Rae minor prophets found a direct stimulus to prophecy and a model for performance in the ritualistic observances of the Alberta prophets. By their own accounts Chi and Naidzo had each been on a personal course toward prophecy for many years. Possibly Chi's prophetic message, focusing as it did on the evils of drink and card playing, crystallized through hearsay reports of the Alberta Prophet reaching him at Marten Lake. (In respect to drink, however, Chi had an impetus closer to home: the death in 1966 of a Lac la Martre man due to drink.) There is no indication that Naidzo encountered even indirect stimulus to prophecy or his prophetic message from hearsay report of the Alberta Prophet. How contrastive the prophetic performances of Chi and Naidzo were to those of Jack and the Alberta model of performance will be brought out below.

The thrust of this study is not to treat of the prophecies of Jack, Naidzo, and Chi as exemplifications of cultural forms or the consequences of particular events or historical circumstances. It is rather to capture the distinctive personal qualities and creativities that each of the three men brought to his prophecy—in becoming a prophet, in his message, in his public performance, and in his prophetic persona—and to situate the prophets in the contexture of authority and authenticity in Dogrib life.

Becoming a Prophet

Naidzo, Chi, and Jack achieved their prophecies by undergoing revelatory experiences in heaven, the heaven where God, Jesus, the apostles, the saints, and angels dwell. Naidzo's and Jack's experiences in the supernal

Christian domain were recurrent. Naidzo traveled the road to heaven "thousands of times," and when he preached an angel stood on each shoulder. Jack too, it seems, went to heaven repeatedly. For Chi, I have only his account of his struggle over many years to achieve initial access to heaven and revelation.

Naidzo's and Chi's accounts of their course toward prophecy show a parallel with the traditional Dogrib understanding of attaining *ink'on* 'medicine power'. The experience that brings *ink'on,* Vital Thomas says, is called dreaming, even if the person is awake.[4] (Recall that a prophet is a dreamer too.) The initial experience with an other-than-human being who empowers one with *ink'on* characteristically takes place in childhood or youth. The empowerment is in the mind, not lodged in any object or action. The beings who empower are called *ink'on,* as is the human person who has *ink'on.* The empowering being tells the initiate when he or she may indicate that he or she has *ink'on.* To speak too soon is to die soon. The voluntary promotion of one's own prophetic preachments contrasts with the handling of one's *ink'on.* One does not volunteer to use one's *ink'on.* One must be asked. Sometimes others must even tease and taunt the curer-adept to get him employ his *ink'on,* "even to save his own life."

Whether Jack had *ink'on* is not clear, though, as we shall see, some Dogribs believed he did. Naidzo had had *ink'on* for hunting and trapping. Vital described Naidzo's name as "meaning something like a trapper." Chi had had *ink'on* for curing and for "playing" *tsinco* (see chap. 7). Both Naidzo and Chi divested themselves of or were divested of these powers as part of becoming a prophet. As with attaining *ink'on,* both had to wait many years after first intimations of their prophecy-to-come before they were "ready" to be prophets.

Chi's Coming to Prophecy

The main features of Chi's progress to prophecy are here extracted from Vital's translation of Chi's account (taped on 2 January 1970):

> From the time I was pretty young, four or five years old, I used to sleep with my dad, in the same bed. That's the time I used to dream about pictures.[5] At the same time I would see a road reaching from earth to heaven. To follow it I needed to read [the first picture on the road]. They told me, "If you can't read this you can't go any further. A fellow that reads and understands is the only person that can go on this road."
>
> Everytime I dreamed I went as far as this picture and came back. The next time, I went as far as that picture and turned back again.

That's what I dreamed, that's the way I started. I don't mean that I dreamed every day, just once in a while. It took so long, so many years. Finally I passed that first picture and went on to the next picture. I dreamed the same thing and came to the same thing again, and every time I awoke I worried. [I asked myself] "What does this mean? I wonder if my dream will come true?"— just worrying. Long after, whenever I dreamed again, it was the same. I saw that road, I saw those pictures. I looked [ahead] to where the road came from. Right at the end of the road [Chi employed the characteristic Dogrib extended-arm-and-hand gesture for indicating something at a distance] there is a building. Finally I saw it with my own eyes.

When I reached that house it was made of glass. The floor itself was so shiny it was like a mirror, and it was so pretty, walls of glass, roof of glass, everything shining—that's the way I dreamed about it.

Then I looked the other way and I saw all the saints. They were so bright and happy. And there was another door. "If you open it here are your wings all piled up for anyone that comes for them," that's what they told me.

And that building was so pretty, just glass, everything shining. And if you look down through the floor, it shows you what you've been doing all your time on earth—how you lived, how many times you make a sacrifice.[6] It shows everything.

I've been to my Father's Place up there. I've seen the wings waiting for us and four drums playing, [but] no ribbons.[7]

That was the way my dreams told me at the time I was growing up. Every time I dreamed I dreamed about the same place. Even after I was grown up I still dreamed about this. Even after I got married, I still dreamed about it. . . .

On the road, any person that comes to the first picture and doesn't know how to read it, he can't go on because he doesn't know how to read. "You can't pass it," that's what they told me. Because you've got to find out which way you're going.

If you don't know how to read, you can't go any farther. But if you pray, pray, each time you may be able to make one step. Pray again, you may get another step. Finally you'll know. And then you will pass the picture. It's pretty hard.

Chi's struggle to proceed along the road to heaven suggests the influence of the pictorial "Catholic ladder" developed by the Oblate missionary Albert Lacombe in the last century and which continued "through the mid-20th century to be for many Subarctic Indians a highly popular and powerful representation of 'salvation history' according to the Roman Catholic faith" (Helm, Rogers, and Smith 1981:fig. 2; for the history of the Catholic ladder, see Hanley 1973). One middle-aged woman found in Chi's preachings an explicit parallel. "What Chi says is just like the Old Testament. He describes the road to heaven and hell and it is just like the picture of the road [Catholic ladder] that the priest has."

Naidzo's Coming to Prophecy

Naidzo the Bear Lake Prophet said that his first experience leading to prophecy came in his youth, before he married. Like Chi, Naidzo had to wait many years until "they" told him to preach. However, neither his first revelatory experience nor subsequent ones came as a dream: "I don't dream."

I expressed the hope to Naidzo that he would recount for me the experiences that brought him to prophecy. My hope was not fulfilled, but not because he refused. When I visited Naidzo, he was in full-flight public performance. It would have been intrusive of me to attempt to control his line of discourse (see below). I had already recorded Vital's account of the prophet's initial revelation as he had told it on an earlier occasion. Vital's recounting of his recollection of Naidzo's story is in the first person, as if Naidzo were speaking:

> When I was young I was so lucky. I was killing all kinds of caribou and fur, whatever. I was well off in those days. Then all of a sudden someone [a divine messenger is implied] came to me and he said, "You are killing too much. If you keep on like this for the rest of your life, at the end of your life you will be sorry. I want to change you, to stop you from killing so much."
>
> He asked me what I thought about that. I said, "It's up to you, because you know the future. It's up to you to do what's right for me." So he said, "When we first start we are going to make you a cripple. How about that?" And I said, "It's up to you. You're the boss. Whatever you say is okay, because I do not want to be sorry in my last days." So then he said, "If we just cripple you you'll still have two arms working and two eyes to see. As long as your eyes are open you won't stop killing. So the best way is to make you blind. What do you think about that?" And I said, "It's up to you. Do what you like. It'll do me good."
>
> He said, "We will make you blind. But before we make you blind we're going to clean out of you all of this *ink'on*, everything you

know." [See part 2; also see D. Smith 1973, 1990; Ridington 1988; Rushforth 1992; and Goulet 1982, 1989, 1990 on *ink'on* as "knowing."] So he walked about and when he got behind me the first time he put his hand just above my head. Then he gave me a little slap on my head and something like ice dripped down me as far as my waist. Then he circled a second time and when he got behind me he gave me another little slap, but harder than the first time, and I felt ice to my knees. Then he said, "This is the last one." And he circled around me again and when he got behind me he gave my head a little heavier slap and all the *ink'on* went out. But some of the *ink'on* was still moving, still alive. Then he got a sack, like . . . [a bellows?]. And he put air inside it like . . . [Vital made an opening and closing motion with hands and arms to indicate he was pumping a sacklike object full of air]. And three times he put air into this sack and each time the air came out with a rush toward the heap of *ink'on,* and on the third time all the *ink'on* disappeared. [The imagery of *ink'on* as a living substance seems unique to Naidzo.]

Then he said to me, "We've cleaned you out good and it will never come back to you." He was standing in front of me and said, "Now that you are cleaned out you look so pitiful." And he put his hand into his pocket and brought out a rosary and, giving it to me, said, "This will help." And he reached in a second time and brought out a kind of holy stone. And the third time he gave me something else holy [Vital had forgotten what the third object was]. And he said, "You will not be sorry. For the rest of your life we will teach you, and when you get old enough you are going to preach."

[The Bear Lake Prophet addressing his audience:] I don't dream. I've seen something like a road to heaven. And twelve persons came there. There were standing on the right side of me, touching me, and someone says, "Do you know these men?" "No." "Well, these are the twelve apostles." And I shake hands with all of them and that is how I started. I bet I've been on that road a thousand times, learning to preach.

According to Vital, Naidzo had said that he "never mentioned a word" of his revelatory experiences until "they" told him he could preach. Naidzo's *ink'on* was for hunting and trapping. His *ink'on* was not good for curing. "A good hunter has no doctor medicine [curing *ink'on*]," said Vital.

Naidzo's account of his being stripped of his *ink'on* occurred early in his visit to Rae during Christmas 1969 (before I arrived in Rae). In June 1969 Vital had recalled other facets of Naidzo's experiences as revealed during his visit the preceding Easter. For one thing, as rendered by Vital:

> Some guys here in Rae say, "I dreamed." With a one-night dream you can't call yourself a prophet. Someone told me, "Pretty soon you're going to become a preacher." It took me four years since they told me I would become a preacher. I just watched. They taught me for four years. In the middle of the summer they came back and said, "We taught you good. Now we think you're able to teach." These guys here with these one-night dreams—anyone that dreams about God and angels, that is for your own good, that is not to talk about.
>
> [Here Vital went on with Naidzo's narrative of his experiences:] They showed me all over, heaven and purgatory and the twelve apostles, sitting in the air, not on the ground. And Jesus suffering for us, with thorns on his head. Finally they took me to heaven and I saw it all. I saw this playground. In heaven they don't have to serve meals. What ever you think about, it is right there. But they told me, "You still come from earth so you cannot eat. We are just showing you how nice it is in heaven and how good we treat one another." So I was just watching. I did not eat with them because I belong to this earthliness. When you finish eating, the plates and cups disappear and right at the door there is a big pile of wings waiting for you. And once you get the wings stuck to your shoulders, you start to smile and run. Ever and ever, no end to it. And Jesus showed me a big door and that is where God is, but "You come from earth so you won't see God." I saw the angels all right but I didn't see God.
>
> I've traveled the road to heaven so many times. I've seen the people up there playing and the platform they are playing on is as big as Great Bear Lake, and *blue!* And the earth up there is shiny, you won't see a piece of rock or hay, and everyone has wings on, playing, thousands of people. [Upon recounting this, Vital exclaimed, "He sure talks! Holy Moses! It don't matter if you listen for two days, you still like to hear more."]

Jack the Rae Prophet

From the two-week visit with other Dogribs to the Alberta prophets in July 1967, Jack returned a prophet in his own right. I have no account of his initiatory revelation. Only a few scraps of information about Jack's mystical or supernal experiences could be garnered, and these from skeptical or hostile persons. He had been to heaven and talked to God, according to one Dogrib. "He says he has talked to an angel," said another. When preaching, angels fly around his shoulders. Vital, though accepting the accounts of heavenly visits by Naidzo and Chi, demurred in the case of Jack: "A living man cannot go to heaven, but Jack goes pretty near every day." A woman commented, "He says that he sees Jesus, but none of us will see Jesus until the Last Judgment." Furthermore, Jack said that right at the entrance to heaven he had seen a big rock with a beaver sitting on it. "There's no beaver in heaven!" said the woman, laughing.

At the community feast on 29 December 1969, following speeches from one of the resident priests, the Old Chief, Barthelemy, and the Dettah Prophet, Jack rose and spoke. He recounted that on the previous evening, just as he was about to say his bedtime prayers, he saw Jesus with "beads" (of the rosary) in his hands. Jesus' hands were about two feet apart (as if holding a skein of yarn for winding). "It was no dream." Jack made the sign of the cross and started to pray and Jesus disappeared. And then Jesus returned and showed Jack the beads again with the same gesture. "I thought Jesus was showing me how to hold the beads so I took my beads and held them the same way." Then Jesus disappeared.

These choppy reports of Jack's revelations—all secondhand except his (taped) account of the vision of Jesus with the beads—do not indicate that Jack's experiences closely conformed to those of the Alberta prophets from whom he borrowed the prophet ritual complex (described below) that he introduced to the Dogribs. According to Goulet, the Alberta "prophets or dreamers in English are the religious elders of the community. They claim and they are credited with the ability to leave their bodies in their sleep, to follow a trail beyond the canopy of heaven and to meet there with the deceased. There, they receive their songs, and the designs for their flags. They come back with visions of things to come in the community" (1982:11).

Goulet's characterization of being a prophet among the Alberta Slavey, enlarged on by Moore and Wheelock (1990:59-86), parallels Ridington's (1981:357) summary of the way to prophecy among the Beavers of British Columbia, a Dene people neighboring on the Alberta Slaveys. No more for Jack than for Naidzo or Chi is there evidence that "the deceased" were significant heavenly encounters that informed Jack's prophecy or that he returned from heaven "with visions of things to come in the community." Nor did Dogrib commentators credit Jack with supernal inspiration for songs or flag emblems: the songs were not his "own," it was said, and the emblems were taken from the Alberta prophets. Lacking Jack's own testimony of his path to prophecy, one can only raise the question of the adequacy of others' reports of his experiences.

2

Message, Performance, and Persona

Message

The three Dogrib prophets were divinely inspired to bring the word and will of Christianity's God to the people. That was the ultimate understanding that underlay the message of each prophet. Although their messages were public pronouncements, addressed to the people, the prophets called on each individual to exercise spiritual and behavioral discipline, effecting personal reformation and, inferentially, the social and moral betterment of the Dogrib people through abandonment of "bad" or injurious practices.

Drinking and card playing were the two evils that the Alberta Prophet and his disciple Jack, and also Chi, excoriated when calling upon the people to reform. Idleness and the neglect of necessary tasks due to incessant card playing had been of concern to thoughtful Dogribs for several years. But they especially acknowledged the prophets' proscription of drinking as addressing a true evil afflicting Dogrib society. The alcohol problem had been mounting since 1959. Before that, the possession or consumption of any form of alcohol was illegal for persons of legal Indian status ("treaty Indians") in the Northwest Territories (N.W.T.). Perforce, alcohol consumption by Dogribs was almost entirely limited to illicit home brew. The 1959 rescission of the N.W.T. law prohibiting the purchase or consumption of alcoholic beverages by Indians was followed within a year by the opening of the road between Rae and Yellowknife, where hard liquor and beer could be bought for immediate consumption or transport back to Rae (Helm and Lurie 1966:79-81).[1]

Within the year before the Alberta Prophet's first visit to Rae at Christmas 1966, three Dogrib men, fathers of families, were lost to alcohol-related deaths. One of the men was from Marten Lake. With the Dogrib community in shock from the deaths, the message of the Alberta

Prophet was the catalyst that brought some Dogribs to forswear drinking and others to moderate and monitor their consumption of alcohol. When Jack assumed prophecy half a year later his followers foreswore drinking. Two years later a sophisticated young nonbeliever credited Jack for a decline in drinking. By 1976, however, it was said that two of the Rae minor prophets, Jack's followers, had started to drink and gamble at cards again.

Probably only the most committed adherents to the messages of Jack and Chi accepted their absolute proscription on card playing. (Chi's vision of the horrors awaiting card players is given below.) Although respectful of Chi as a prophet, Vital could not accede to his ban on cards, so he sought the priest's assurance that "a little card playing is alright." (In fact, Vital did not observe Chi's proscription of drinking either.)

Jack endorsed the traditional Dogrib hand game with its attendant wagers; he had seen the hand game played in heaven. (In our study of the Dogrib hand game, Lurie and I note that "the hand game, both in the eyes of the Dogribs and of the uninvolved observer, presents none of the social problems of gambling with cards" [1966:81].) As another form of recreation spiritually acceptable to Jack, the traditional bow-and-arrow game was taken up in the bush settlements of the *et'at'in,* the Dogrib regional band from which came the main group of Jack's adherents. Chinese checkers was one white-derived game that received Jack's approbation. A distinctive component of his prophecy was his animadversions on white intrusions and pernicious influences in Dogrib life. His mode of social and political resistance to the white presence is sketched in the section on performance, below.

Naidzo said that a person who wants to be happy on this earth should not drink or gamble at cards. These activities are not good. But his concern about this behavior appeared to be very muted compared to that of Chi and Jack. Naidzo's message did not stress specific "wrong" activities such as drinking and card playing. Rather, he emphasized actively good spiritual and social behavior.

In a sharp departure from Christian dogma, sex as a potentially potent source of sin was not a theme in the prophets' messages. (Dogribs reported quite the contrary in Jack's case, of which more below.) Naidzo "talks about women," according to Vital, but in this vein: "Naidzo says it is not much of a sin, because a man is made for a woman and a woman is made for a man. Like Adam and Eve. God made Adam and Eve, but still they were sad. They didn't know what to do. So God made them think about how to have children. So it happened, and all the people [in the world] come from two persons."

The prophets shared the encompassing message that calls upon the people to live in accord with God and Jesus, to lead a better life. Only from Naidzo and Chi, however, were direct preaching statements recorded. Both emphasized that one should reflect on one's self and one's behavior, exercise self-control, and give thought to what one is doing to make sure one does right and good at all times. Keep God's word, think of God, believe in God. Through self-discipline and keeping God's word one can save one's soul. Chi said, "Ask God to keep you away from that which is forbidden." "To steal, cheat, talk behind someone's back is bad," said Naidzo, "but the worst thing you can do is to kill somebody, whether it is by *ink'on* or with a club." Do no harm to anyone. Naidzo, however, also stressed that one should smile, laugh, joke, because "that comes from heaven—mean and cranky comes from the devil."

The affirmative tenor of Naidzo's message was demonstrated in a formal speech he directed to me during my first visit to him:

> Thanks for your gift. Anything a person gives is not only to me, it is God's, because if you help the poor that's like you are making a sacrifice for God. It won't show on this earth that you give to the poor. It is only after you die that God will tell you how many times you helped the poor and how kind you were. If you keep on doing kindness to people it's like you are putting something aside. When you die and are in heaven you will be happy for ever and ever. Any person that helps me and takes pity on me, I am going to pray for him. I am going to help him to see what I see in heaven. Any person that listens to my story, what I say about heaven, must think about himself [reflect on his own behavior and spiritual condition]. Nobody is going to help him out, he's got to try to get to heaven on his own. Make sacrifices, God is going to help you. You have to think, you have to ask yourself, "Why did I do this? How long have I been doing this? Now I'm going to change myself, along the ways the old man [Naidzo] is talking." That's why I [have come from Fort Franklin to] meet you people here. To talk about God in your own life. Some people talk nice but they still don't care much about their own soul. Everyone has a soul and we are all going to come to the Last Judgment. Before that time I have come here to explain that to all of you. I hope you will take my word and try to save your soul. You won't be sorry for ever and ever. [excerpts of Vital's translation of my tape recording]

Performance

Contrastive qualities of character and personal style, to be addressed below, infused the public presentations of each of the three prophets. For the moment, the focus is more narrow: What did each do as he enacted his role as prophet? In this respect the distinction between Jack, on one hand, and Naidzo and Chi, on the other, could hardly be more clear cut. As one woman commented, "Chi and Naidzo are just the same; Jack is different." Jack introduced and led a program of religious ritual that encompassed group dance. Naidzo and Chi were gurus, venerable religious teachers, offering inspired knowledge and guidance to those who would heed them. They only preached, they did not enjoin cultic observances and performances upon their believers or adherents. In contrast to Jack, they had neither ritual emblems nor equipage, nor, with the exception of their prophet songs, a ceremonial act.

Several prophet songs—songs speaking of angels, "heaven [sky] people"—were an integral part of Jack's ritual performances. Some said that his songs were not his own: he had borrowed the songs of the Alberta prophet cult. Vital thought that one of Jack's songs came from Harry Natéa ("Little Prophet"), a Slavey who was performing as a prophet perhaps fifty years before (see chap. 3, "Earlier Prophets").

It was unusual that at the time of his visits to Rae Naidzo had no prophet songs. Only in 1973 was it reported that Naidzo had three songs, but "not many have heard them" because he revealed his songs only shortly before he died in Franklin earlier that year.

Although he did not sing them on his one visit to Rae at Christmas 1969, Chi was known to have two or three prophet songs of his own composition. At Easter 1969, when the Alberta Prophet, Naidzo, and Jack were together in Rae, two men from Marten Lake sang one of Chi's songs. Vital, whose appreciation may have been heightened because of his distaste for Jack, recounted:

> I heard one of Chi's songs at Eastertime. Jeez, it was good, Holy Moses! At first the Marten Lake men said they wouldn't sing his song. But then they started singing it, hitting the drum, to show how good the song was. Holy Moses, a real one! As soon as they hit the drums it was just like the drums were shaking, they sounded so good! And Jack thinks that he is going to sing good [in competition with Chi's song] but then he got shy-like. He hit the drum, but nobody moved. With Chi's song everybody joined in [dancing] and in no time there was a big circle. I heard Chi's song just once so I don't know the words, but the song speaks of angels anyway.

Unlike Jack, who had a house in Rae, Naidzo and Chi were visitors to the settlement. Naidzo's visits constituted major public occasions. Both Naidzo and Chi stayed as guests in Rae households. During his three visits—Easter 1969, Christmas-New Year's 1969-1970, and Easter 1971—Naidzo resided with the parental family of his new daughter-in-law. On his single visit to Rae at Christmas 1969, Chi and his wife stayed with the household of Barthelemy, the elder who had been instrumental in bringing the Alberta Prophet to Rae.

To the households where the prophets stayed the people contributed food when they visited and brought gifts of tobacco and money to the prophet. Apparently Jack received clothing, a tent, and other equipment. "The people give Jack everything—pants, white shirt, drymeat, dryfish. Jack puts it on the table in his house. Anyone can take it." (In a detractor's opinion, Jack had simply found a way of "getting everything free from the people.")

Three months later, Vital described Naidzo's first three-week visit to Rae at Easter 1969. "Every morning we go over, and there is a full house. People bring food and they [the women of the household] cook meals and at the same time the old man is preaching. Those people get fed and at the same time more people come in. It's a full house 'til midnight." My first visit to Naidzo, during the Christmas season of 1969, confirmed that account. Excerpts from my field notes follow:

> With a bitter wind at our backs, Vital and I started out at about a quarter to one. When we entered the house where Naidzo is staying perhaps 12 adults were there, mostly older men and a few women, plus the requisite small children. Naidzo was seated at the far end of the house on a foam mattress with sleeping rolls piled behind him. He was sitting cross-legged, Buddha-fashion, with all the air of holding court. He is a man of great presence, very handsome, with grey-white hair coming down to his collar line. One of his sightless eyes is concealed by the sunken closed eyelid.
>
> We went through the routine of greeting that most entrants did. This was to go up and shake hands, setting our gift of food before him, and speak to him. He holds one's hand for a goodly time in a firm clasp. After an explanation of who I was, the old man shook my hand vigorously and held on for a minute while he joshed. As Vital had told me, the old fellow "likes to joke about women." He said something to me to the effect of my staying the night. I joked back that if his stories were good I would probably want to and besides my cabin is cold. Laughter from all. He tended to stroke or feel the hand in his as he talked to each greeter, and he repeatedly

Naidzo, Christmas 1969 at Rae.

made some sort of risqué or flirtatious comment to young unmarried women, including prepubescent girls. (He probably slipped up on my age because my hand was soft, like a girl's.)

People came, perhaps 40 in all, and went during the four hours that we were there, especially during the first couple of hours. Some younger or less consequential men just drifted in on the outskirts. About half the people who entered came up and greeted Naidzo formally. Several pressed a dollar bill (perhaps more) in his hand as they greeted him. Also, he received about four packs of cigarettes. Some addressed him as *ehtse* (grandfather). Many of the persons spoke to Naidzo at some length and he replied at even greater length. Several entire families greeted him and were greeted formally. One family was from Hay Lakes-Meander River, the father was wearing the green jacket that signifies an adherent of the Alberta prophet movement. A number of Dogribs from Dettah were there and several visitors from Marten Lake came in.

The old man is indefatigable. He speaks in a strong full voice. By his voice, one would never guess that he is close to 80. Literally, from about one o'clock to four he ceased interaction only long enough to be once guided outdoors to the latrine. He held the floor the whole time. If anyone spoke at moderate length to him, he replied in extenso. For my benefit he narrated two lengthy legends [one, the oral history of the confrontation of the Dogrib Edzo and the Yellowknife Akaitcho, is featured in Helm and Gillespie 1981]. He must have been talking for several hours before we came in, yet he showed no signs of fatigue.

There were jokes and laughter interspersed between his sermons, narrations, and orations. In fact, he tended to evoke laughter even in discourse that was obviously not simply an amusing anecdote. The men and women sat (on the floor, as customary) absolutely rapt as soon as he launched into any kind of an account. Eyes were fixed on him. No one whispered or made an aside to his neighbor. Only the small children and the opening and closing of the door as people came and went broke the spell. He indulged in many interchanges of jokes with the men sitting around him. There was much laughter and pleasure throughout the whole session.

* * *

About four o'clock a dinner was served. As is usual at Dogrib feasts, lengths of oilcloth were rolled out on the floor and stewed rice along with bread, bannock, jam and butter was served. The old man was given a big plate of fried meat as well. Naidzo led the prayers at the meal, with the double signing of the cross before the meal and again at the finish. The brother of Naidzo's deceased wife served as kind of *k'awo* ('boss') in directing the young men who rolled out the oilcloths, set the "table," and served the food. Those few who had been unable to crowd around the sides of the oilcloth on the floor were served once the first bunch said their "amen." There were opening and closing prayers at the meal of the second set of persons as well.

* * *

In summary, along with the pleasure and pleasantries of the assembly, the respect and attention shown to Naidzo was notable.

One woman spoke to him with such fervor that I wondered if she was appealing to him for salvation. Men in their fifties and sixties hung on his words as if spellbound, as one man and then another sat directly facing the Prophet and took turns in punctuating Naidzo's speeches at short intervals with the requisite *ehn!,* the 'yes' with which one responds to the words of another. [For Dene patterns of communicative interaction, including the use of *yes,* see Scollon and Scollon 1984.]

On two subsequent, and briefer, visits to Naidzo within the following week there were fewer persons present, more interchange among them, and the sense of Naidzo holding court or keeping his audience in a sustained grip was lacking. Naidzo again, however, displayed his range of discourse. He drew on his repertoire of legends and lore, recounting, among other things, the legend of the woman who turned into the copper deposits near the Coppermine River (cf. Petitot 1888:567–71) and of the animal-monster that lived in the rock under a high cliff on Great Bear Lake but burst forth when the pitchblende miners began blasting. Said Naidzo, "When the white man smells money, he'll dig anywhere. Us, we'd never get close." Naidzo discoursed on schooling and the consequent loss of bush skills by the young people and spoke appreciatively of the services supplied at Fort Franklin by the welfare state. He urged his audience to make the sign of the cross to protect themselves from things in the night. The first signing of the cross stops a danger at arm's length and the second signing causes that danger to shoot off in an instant. He cautioned that if one dreams about God or heaven one should keep it to oneself. "Someday, you may get help, but don't tell it to anyone because others might laugh." One should smile, laugh, be friendly, because God likes that.

In performance Chi lacked Naidzo's virtuosity as a source of legend and lore and of commentary on times past and present. And he notably lacked Naidzo's social ease, expansiveness, and affability. As a prophet, Chi, as I observed him, limited himself to his visionary experiences and his prophetic message. Since so much of Chi's message is reflective of his persona, it is more appropriately treated in a separate section (see "Persona," below).

After Jack returned from Alberta in the summer of 1967 as a prophet, there were prophet performances, preaching, and drumming-singing and dancing at Jack's house—"steady for two weeks," according to one account. Jack enjoined his adherents to wear something white, and his male followers could be identified by white shirts. From a flagpole at

Jack's house flew a flag bearing a symbol, given him by the Alberta Prophet, which Jack attempted to persuade others to pray to when passing.

From early in his prophecy, Jack enunciated resentment of and resistance to white presence and pressures in Dogrib life—the church and its priests apparently excepted. His unsuccessful call in the summer of 1968 for a Dogrib boycott of the election, from among white candidates, of a member of parliament from the Northwest Territories was about the only form of overt rejection of the Euro-Canadian power system feasible at that time. In the main, he could only attempt to cordon off the internal Dogrib world from the intrusion of whites and their ways. His theme that white people would "laugh at the Indians"—that is, react contemptuously or with disrespect if allowed to observe or experience Indian activities— was no imaginary issue, and it struck a responsive chord in some. The tourism of sorts that the highway now brought to Rae—whites who came to view the settlement and the seasonal festivities of treaty time—could only exacerbate that anxiety. More particularly, Jack strove to guard the sanctity and solemnity of his prophet performances from whites or white-style observation. He prohibited the use of cameras and tape recorders even by fellow Indians. The "news" from Fort Norman was that, in the eyes of those local Dene, he and his minor-prophet companions from Rae far overstepped the line when they forebade the local priest to tape their songs at treaty festivities when they visited in August 1970.

In the greater Dogrib community Jack met with little success in enforcing his dictum to "keep whites away." An old lady brought a couple of touring white men to Jack's prophet dance at his own house. Even individuals respectful or convinced of Jack's authority as a prophet apparently felt free to make their own decisions about how they handled relations with whites, at least on a person-by-person basis.

Jack held frequent prophet dances (my term for the the ritual group dance and associated observances he led) at his house in the first year of his prophecy (1967). Since the space in a government-built house such as he had is modest, the number of persons who could squeeze in was restricted. Public attention and attendance at a prophet dance surely peaked on Sunday, 30 June 1968, when Jack orchestrated the ceremony at a dance corral (my term) he and his followers had just prepared near Marian River Village, a bush hamlet about two hours by canoe from Rae. In mid-afternoon, a straggling flotilla of canoes, loaded to the gunwales with humanity, set out from Rae for the dance site. A substantial contingent of Dogribs from the hamlet of Dettah, near Yellowknife, would also have attended, had word reached them in time. But a wire from Jack, received there on Sunday, led the Dettah folk to understand

Marian River Village. The cleared circle of the prophet dance "corral" shows at the upper right portion of this point extending into Marian Lake. 1976.

that the dance was to be held at Rae on Monday night and Tuesday morning. When they arrived at that time at Rae, some coming the many miles by canoe, they found nothing happening.

Perhaps 300 people (including children) attended the prophet ceremony at Marian River Village that Sunday. Attendance was not limited to persons taking Jack's prophecy seriously. But over a hundred adults, by my crude estimate, demonstrated their solemn commitment to the purpose of the occasion by making a personal oblation at the start of the ceremony. The following account of the prophet ceremony is adapted from my field notes.[2]

The Prophet Ceremony of Jack the Rae Prophet

Marian River Village, where the ceremony was held, is at the far end of Marian Lake, the northernmost extension of Great Slave Lake. The residents of this village, a segment of the *et'at'in,* were said to be enthusiastic followers of Jack. (Jack himself is an *et'at'in.*) Behind the several log cabins and tents that lined the shore, a traveler approaching by canoe could see, over a rise, dip, and rise again of granite outcrop, seven white flags (one for each minor prophet plus Jack?) waving above the scrub bush. Farther to the west, two more white flags on poles were visible.

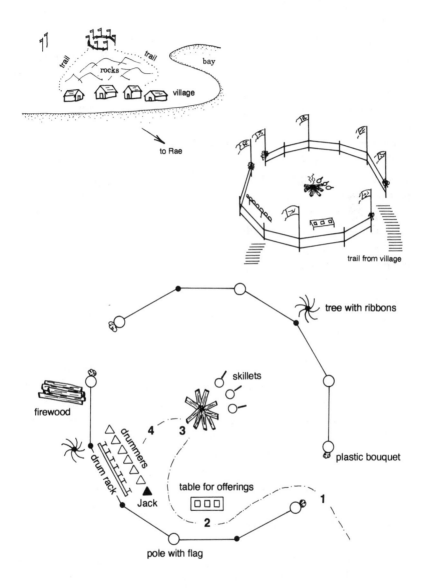

Figure 2. The Prophet Dance at Marian River Village: Site and Arrangements. Those making oblations (1) genuflected and signed the cross upon entering the "corral," (2) placed offerings in the basins on the table, and (3) usually went to the fire to dispose of the wrapping from the oblations. A few women (4) went before the drummer and signed the cross.

Two trails led over the brief passage from the hamlet to the site of the ceremony (see fig. 2). At the site the bush had been cleared for several hundred yards around. In the center of the clearing had been erected a large twelve-sided corral (about seventy-five to a hundred feet across) made of long, freshly peeled poles. The north and south sides were open, a pole's length across, as entrances to the corral. The floor of the corral had been leveled and smoothed for dancing. The construction had just been completed; this was the first ceremony to be held in it. It was said to be identical to those erected by the Alberta prophets.

On either side of the two entrances were tall poles from which flew decorated white flags. To each pole at about chest height was attached a plastic bouquet of pink flowers and green leaves, tied with ribbon. Three other poles placed along the fence of the corral served as flagpoles as well. Each flagpole flew a white flag with a design on it and with short ribbons flowing from it. Each emblem was different. One design appeared to be the heart of Jesus flanked by two crosses. In the center of the corral was a log fire. Beside the fire sat three skillets, a pound of lard melting in each. To one side within the corral a low board table held three plastic washbasins (depositories for offerings) and, supported by uprights, a horizontal bar of peeled pole served as a rack for the drums of the Prophet and the six minor-prophet drummers. The seven beribboned tambourine drums used in the ceremony had been newly made for the occasion. In the course of a "sermon," Jack explained the motifs that should have been drawn on the drumheads but which were not executed for lack of time. As the drummers performed, a rosary dangled over the forearm that held the drum. When not in use, the drums were hung on the rack and the rosaries were usually hung with them.

Three kinds of ceremonial events took place within the corral: an offerings ritual, which occurred only at the beginning; sacred songs and sermons (my designations); and group dancing. The second and third events were repeated in sequence.

About 7 P.M. three rifle shots signaled people to come to the corral. The ritual of offerings initiated the events of the evening. By the end of the offerings ritual, over a hundred adults were within the corral. Jack and the six other drummers maintained a steady drumming-singing until all those who chose to make an oblation had passed through the line. Once dancing began, other persons freely entered the corral.

Participants carrying out the oblation ritual came in the south entrance of the corral. Before one or another of the plastic bouquets tied to the flagpoles the worshipper thrice genuflected and signed the cross three times before arising. Upon reaching the table, each person repeated the set of genuflections-with-crossings before each of the three plastic washbasins, placing an offering of tobacco in the first basin, a piece of bannock (baking-powder bread) in the second, and tobacco again in the third. Most persons then went to the fire to dispose, in a casual manner, the paper that had wrapped the offerings. A few women then went before the drummers and crossed themselves. One woman directed three full genuflections-with-crossings to the Prophet.

When offerings had ceased, the Prophet led the other drummers to the oblation table. His wife, who had been standing beside him, accompanied them, as did two or three additional men. The walk to the table was the first time the drumming-singing had ceased.

First in line, the Prophet moved beyond the table. His wife followed him to a point behind the first basin. The others were in line behind her. The slow drumming-singing began again. The wife of the Prophet performed a set of three genuflections-with-crossings before each basin, the Prophet moving slowly one pace sidewise to accommodate her sidewise step. The drummers followed. After she had completed the three "stations," Bartholemy took one basin, the Prophet's wife took a second, and one of the minor prophets took the third. With the drum-singing continuing, the Prophet, the basin-carriers, and the drummers moved slowly in a clockwise circle to the center of the corral and the fire. Men standing on the sidelines stepped forward and threw the three skilletsful of lard onto the fire. As great flames leaped, the three basin carriers threw the offerings of tobacco and bannock into the fire.

Then began the second kind of event in the total ceremony. Facing across the fire toward the table whence the offerings had come, the Prophet sang a slow wailing song, accompanying himself by striking the frame of his drum. (This is the common way for men singing solo.) The other drummers kept time by beating in the air with their stick hand.

After singing for a few minutes, the Prophet began to speak. His sermon, I was later informed, was about the designs on the flags. The Prophet explained the significance or symbolism of each of the motifs, which were designs (according to observers) taken from the Alberta cult.

After perhaps four or five minutes, the Prophet ceased to speak. Then Bartholemy began to speak in a strong hortatory tone. As soon as he began, Jack assumed a casual attitude and lit a cigarette. Bartholemy spoke for perhaps three to five minutes. Then the Prophet spoke again, then Bartholemy, then an alternation of exhortation by Bartholemy and the Prophet to the men in the corral. (I was unable later to get any account of the subjects addressed.) Throughout the speeches of the Prophet and Bartholemy, the men gave the customary murmur of assent.

The Prophet and the minor-prophet-drummers returned to place their backs to the drum rack and to begin the next episode: the "sacred" drum dance.

There were five short drum dances, each one lasting about three minutes. The Prophet and his cohort of minor prophets did the drumming and singing for all five. Later in the evening, when the drum dancing took on a more secular tone, Jack danced to other drummers as he did in some of the later tea dance sessions. To my untutored ear, the drum dance melodies seemed like ones I had heard at secular events in the past. (But were the words new and sacred rather than secular?) As the people danced, they did not form a single line of dancers pressed front to back (as is ordinarily the case in a drum dance), but were two or three, and later three and four, deep, packed close together around the fire. (Is this the Alberta style?) At the end of each of these short dances, the dancers crossed themselves, some three times.

After the set of five drum dances, tea dancing began, the people forming the tea dance circling around the fire. In the tea dance, group song is the only accompaniment; the people dance shoulder to shoulder, facing toward the center of the circle (Helm and Lurie 1966: chaps. 2, 3). The people had kept a certain air of solemnity during the five drum dances. The customary sound of approval given after a dance, usually a joyous "heay-heay," was subdued, more like a low "yes" *(enh)*. In the tea dancing, however, the final approval sounded in the usual enthusiastic way, adding to the impression that the tea dancing lacked the religious overtones of the drum dancing. The tea dances were short, perhaps three or four minutes each. During secular festivities they usually last many more minutes. After about five tea dances were performed in this first session, the Prophet called for attention in order to introduce a session of drumming-singing by visitors from the south.

Three Dene visitors from Alberta were called forward by the Prophet. The three men, each garbed in a bright green zippered jacket that signified a member of the Alberta prophet cult, came from the opposite side of the corral, and each was followed by his wife, who stood beside him. Each man selected a drum from the drum rack. They played three dances. The tunes were noticeably different from Dogrib melodies, and the visitors' drum technique on the first stanzas was also different from the Dogrib style. After expressions of thanks and appreciation to the visitors by Barthelemy and Prophet Jack, the other Dogrib prophet-drummers lined up with the Prophet and sang a second set of sacred songs, led by the Prophet. These were followed by another "sermon" from the Prophet. Then drum dancing began again. By this time, no one could be seen signing the cross after the dance. There was a general air of secular pleasure. The group danced several dances to the drumming-singing that lasted about thirty minutes. At about 11:30 tea dancing began again. By midnight the family with whom I had traveled to the ceremony were preparing to return to Rae, so my observations ended.[3]

At the prophet dance at Marian River Village Jack announced a plan to build a similar corral at Rae. It did not materialize. During the next year or two other prophet dances were held at the Marian River dance grounds, but they apparently drew substantially fewer numbers than the inaugural dance.

Persona

In the mode of prophet performance, Jack, as a cultic leader, contrasted with Naidzo and Chi as gurus. As a public personality, each prophet had his own distinctive configuration of character. In one broad respect, however, Naidzo and Jack shared a quality lacking in Chi. Although the manner of action and content of performance of each were distinctive one from the other, both Naidzo and Jack were socially assertive. They sought and enjoyed the spotlight; their travels to expand their audiences is evidence alone. As prophets, each presented an expansive persona. Shyness is a quality that no observer would have ascribed to Naidzo or Jack. But this is the very attribute that Chi saw in himself and that others saw in him. Bereft of social ebullience, Chi's presentation of self as a person and a prophet showed a constricted, uncertain, threatened quality. Recall his anxious struggle to "read the picture" that would allow him to follow the road to heaven. Other information about Chi, provided by him and others, is also revealing.

Even before my field partner Nancy Lurie and I arrived at Marten Lake in 1959, we knew of Chi as a medicine man to whom a young couple and the wife's parents—our companions on the two-night canoe trip to Marten Lake—were taking an ailing infant. Statements by Chi's fellow community members between 1959 and 1962 revealed that he was both a kind of herbalist, applying tobacco or gathered plants to injuries, and in the case of illnesses a singing doctor (curer by *ink'on*). Holding his rosary, he sang over ailing persons, usually giving them at the conclusion a Catholic holy picture, accompanied at least once by a bottle of patent medicine. It was said that the animal from which he gained his *ink'on* as a singing doctor was a small duck *(det'oan)*. A Marten Lake resident commented in 1969 that Chi had quit curing several years before. "From

In fast water en route to Lac la Martre, 1959.

now on I'll preach," Chi had said, "but I won't do medicine." Also, as one of the "medicine men" (i.e., men with *ink'on*) at Marten Lake, Chi in former times had performed in *tsinco* enactments (see part 2).

Before the late 1960s, when air transport became common, Indians traveled between Marten Lake and Rae by canoe-and-portage in summer and by dog team in winter. Like other old men living in bush settlements, Chi did not travel to Rae for trade but entrusted his furs and purchase list to younger male relatives. But, according to Vital, Chi had not been to Rae for many, many years, because:

> Chi pretty near got in jail once. [At the time, Vital was special constable—interpreter, factotum, and guide—to the Royal Canadian Mounted Police posted at Rae.] That's why he never shows himself in town. When his stepdaughter came back from [Fort Resolution mission] school [this would place the incident in the mid-1920s], she got crazy, talked silly, and was telling all kinds of stories. She said she had a baby from her stepfather, and that started it. The police wanted to know what happened to the baby, so they were after Chi trying to prove what happened to the baby. The people [of Marten Lake] and Chi said his stepdaughter was silly, that she didn't know what she was talking about. But the mounties said that

Winter aspect of the summer canoe route from Rae to Lac la Martre. The falls (frozen in this picture) is a major portage. The winter dog sled route is more direct. 1959.

something must be there, there's always something behind such a story. The police were after him for two weeks or a month trying to find him. I was working for the mounties at that time and they were taking Chi back and forth. Finally, Chi was crying. But I don't know what finally happened.

Chi did come to Rae in the summer of 1959, when the Roman Catholic mission was celebrating its centenary and encouraging all outlying Dogribs to gather at Rae. The next time Chi visited Rae was at Christmas 1969, when the Marten Lakers, now traveling by chartered ski plane, came en masse to Rae to see the Bear Lake Prophet. At that time I was able to record Chi's account of his struggle to prophecy and his sermon against drink and cardplaying.

Other than Vital, who accompanied me, there were no men visiting Chi when I visited him, only a couple of older women. Chi's wife was with him, and, before I left, her female cousin from Dettah came to visit. My prior acquaintance with Chi was fortunate, for toward the end of the interview he stated, "If it wasn't for you coming to visit me, I would not say a word." Two days before, "somebody" had told Chi, "Don't talk too much, because it is not [may not be?] a true story." (I later discussed that statement with Vital, who thought that the somebody was not a real person: "I think a dream told him.") So, Chi said, until the interview he had not spoken that day or all day before.

When Chi spoke of his visionary experiences, he started with bowed head and clasped hands. During his narrative he gestured to accent his points, but at no time did he really look at anyone; rather, he stared into space. His discourse was very repetitive; a stripped-down account follows:

Pray and beg God to give you the strength to be good and ask the Blessed Virgin to help you. Keep away from that which is bad. In the old days people made home brew. Now some people are drinking hard liquor. That's no good, it's just like killing your soul. If you look into your cup [of liquor] you don't see what I see with my two eyes. It goes like this [the curled fingers of his upturned hand wiggle]—working. It becomes like worms. We call in *kon ti* [fire water]. That means it is just like fire. The more you take the more you want. It will kill your soul. Who will help you? Only the Devil, forever and ever without end. If you are too full, you start to vomit. And everytime you vomit, your tongue comes out [indicates a length of about one foot] and on the end are red flames. I wish I could show you right in your cup the way it works, and your tongue getting longer with flames. If you could see that, I don't think you would touch any more drink.

It is the same with cards. They are no good. If you play too often, pretty soon there's nothing but cards on your mind. When you play, the pictures on the cards come to life and start to laugh at you. They tangle up in your sleeves. You won't feel it, but your whole body will become covered with cards. [Chi's gestures indicated a writhing substance or entity that earlier a woman auditor had described as "like a serpent."] The more you play, the longer it [the writhing substance] gets. Finally it is going to wrap all around your body and cover your whole body, legs and all, and you will die. If we don't see, we don't believe, but I have seen it with my own eyes. Every time you fan out your cards and the face cards show, the faces start to laugh. Like the joker, with big white teeth. The more the cards laugh, the longer the teeth get, but you don't see it. This story I'm telling you about card games and liquor, it's not just me. [Other] prophets will tell you it's no good.

Once you die, your flesh will become earth again, but your soul won't die. Your soul is going to reach God, and at the end of the world each person's soul will come to him again. At the end of the world you'll hear all this thunder and God Himself will be coming with a flute [*detcin-ci* 'peeled willow whistle'] and that whistle will sound so loud that the thunder is nothing. That flute to wake all the dead is going to shake all the earth, it's so loud. Then it will be too late. What have you done? You are going to be judged. Everyone will be scared then, with tears in their eyes. If you are bad, you will go to the left. If you are good, you will stand on the right side. [from Vital's translation of a tape recording]

Chi's visions of the consequence of drinking liquor and playing cards communicate a horror and revulsion that are notably absent from Naidzo's prophetic discourse. An unsure, possibly fearful, quality to Chi's conception of his own visionary experiences and of his relations with his fellows emerged following upon his account of his many years of struggle to "read the picture" in his revelatory dream of prophecy. He went on to say:

Anywhere I go, I do not join in with everybody. I like to keep apart from people. That's the way I have been until now. I don't like to bother anyone or anyone to bother me. Any time I came to Rae for Treaty or whatever, you would never see me around with the bunch. I was too shy to show myself. That is why I hid my dream from others, at the same time being too shy to show myself. That's the way I raised my children. I don't want to bother anybody, I don't want to get into trouble. So I hid myself, like right until now.

In 1960, along with some two dozen other Marten Lake Dogribs, Chi took the Rorschach and Thematic Apperception tests (which I administered under rushed conditions and without the aid of an adequate interpreter). There was surprise expressed within the Marten Lake community that Chi was willing to participate. I certainly do not argue that even under ideal conditions of administration, projective test protocols always adequately or reliably reveal personality configurations, especially in respect to the evaluation of an individual rather than the identification of group modalities. In light, however, of what his discourse reveals of his self-perception and the quality of his prophetic experiences, Chi's characterization adduced from his projective test records takes on a special interest. In 1963 George A. DeVos analyzed Chi's protocols blind (except for age, sex, and family connections). The following statements are drawn from DeVos' analysis:

On the Rorschach none of Chi's responses indicates any affective enrichment. There is a complete lack of responsiveness to the color of the cards. The overriding characteristic of his personality manifest in the Rorschach is extreme constriction and guardedness. There is some evidence for a type of shading shock, of proneness

to paralyzing anxiety. In the Thematic Apperception Test [TAT] we
again find evidence of his constriction and unproductive approach.
Nevertheless, in the TAT stories he does tend to perceive situations
evocative of emotions of pity and tenderness in judging other
individuals. He is not alone in such stories, since these feelings are
characteristic of a number of Marten Lake Dogrib records and are
far more easily evoked than stories dwelling on aggressive themes.
In respect to the expression of emotions between individuals, Chi
avoids giving stories of aggression on TAT cards where they are
usually invoked [in cross-cultural testing] but chooses, nevertheless,
to see situations of antagonism between man and woman or man
and man on other cards.

In summary, the tests indicate that Chi is a highly constricted
individual who shows some potentiality for introceptive concerns
with human feelings and emotions. He has a streak of tenderness in
him and is prone to the expression of pity over sadness found in
other human beings. On the other hand he is not incapable of an
expression of anger or disharmony. Generally speaking, however,
there is a lack of active emotional responsiveness. One feels that
both his sympathy and his anger are passively experienced, rather
than acted upon. Chi's projective record exemplifies usual features
found in the Dogrib records, the paucity of expression and the lack
of delineation of role relationships of individuals, one to the other.
[DeVos' analysis is in my possession; for a summary and com-
parative assessment of the Dogrib projective tests data, based on
two chapters of an uncompleted manuscript by Helm and DeVos,
see Honigmann 1975:555-59.]

Apparently Chi never visited Rae again. In 1979, when we had our last
conversation about prophets, Vital commented that "the only one they
mention is Chi. Only if some stranger from Rae or Rae Lakes visits Lac
la Martre, only then Chi speaks about religion. People at Marten Lake got
tired, they won't listen to him, that's what they say."

* * *

In 1914 (Osgood 1932:33) a Dogrib regional band leader known as the
Bear Lake Chief (see part 2) and his followers abandoned Rae as a point
of trade and thereafter traded into Fort Norman (and later Franklin) in the
Great Bear Lake area. Naidzo was one of those followers.[4] Born (or at
least baptized) in 1890, Naidzo would have been about twenty-four years
old at the time of the withdrawal. "So," he said, "since then we [the Bear
Lake Chief's band] have never been to Rae again." In consequence, Vital

could offer little information on Naidzo's personal history. He was recognized to have been a great trapper, hunter, and traveler in his youth, as he himself attested. He was joyously reunited with an aged friend from the Edge-of-the-Woods band upon his return to Rae. Although not of the Edge-of-the Woods group himself, Naidzo was said to have "traveled all over" in his youth, establishing many friendships.

When and by what physical causes Naidzo became crippled and blind are unknown. An Oblate priest formerly resident at Fort Franklin estimated that Naidzo had been blind for perhaps twenty-five years before his visit to Rae. Naidzo's "suffering" from his afflictions drew respect from the Dogribs and, as Naidzo himself believed, validated him as a true (authentic) prophet. Yet, Naidzo's own presentation of his attainment of prophecy evinced none of the "pitiful" (a favorite Dogrib expression) and uncertain struggle that his age-mate Chi experienced. Naidzo seemed downright cheerful in comparison. "It's up to you. Do what you like. It'll do me good," Naidzo had responded to the being who told him that he must become blind and crippled in order to become a prophet. Whatever physical and emotional suffering or psychological stress Naidzo may have undergone as his afflictions came upon him were submerged under the ebullience and gusto for life and sociability that he evinced in these, his last years. The tensions evidenced by Chi and Jack could not be discerned in Naidzo.

As a social personality Naidzo was outgoing, confident, knowledge-able, and quick to establish personal connections with others. As Vital described him, "It has been fifty years since he has been in Rae, but he knows who shakes hands with him and he knows their dad and mother. He says, 'I saw your dad going with the York boats' or 'I knew your dad, we hunted caribou in the summertime.'"

Naidzo projected an active intelligence. He was a goldmine of native legend and oral history. His narrations were extensive, coherent, and delivered with dramatic force even as teased out through tape recorder and interpreter. (He sometimes slipped into the Bearlake dialect.) He seemed to enjoy himself thoroughly and to appreciate his own per-formance. And markedly throughout the course of his sermons and legendary and historical accounts, Naidzo offered gaiety in his public performance, so contrastive to the styles of Chi and Jack. Apparently some Dogribs were put off by Naidzo's mode of "telling all kinds of stories and making jokes about women." But Naidzo in turn was put off by the unrelentingly solemn preaching of Jack and the Alberta Prophet and by the latter's "scolding" (and perhaps by competition from them) when the three prophets were together in Rae at Easter 1969. "It's like they spoiled my fun," he reportedly said.

Jack was thirty years younger than Naidzo and Chi. He became a prophet at the age of forty-eight—mature but fifteen to twenty years removed from becoming an elder in Dogrib society. Since I was blocked from direct interaction with Jack after his assumption of prophecy—not so much by the no-whites stance he proclaimed as by Vital's resolute opposition and hostility toward him—I can only skirt around the edges of observation and information on his personality and character. Local perspectives on Jack's behavior were gained mainly from bilinguals skeptical of or hostile to Jack as a prophet. I am unable to do Jack the justice of presenting aspects of his self-perception such as Chi and Naidzo allowed me.

Although I had carried out fieldwork at Rae in the summer of 1962, it was not until Nancy Lurie and I returned in June 1967 that, out of the large Dogrib population there, we became aware of Jack. Jack and other visitors to the Alberta Prophet had introduced "feeding the fire" at public feasts—a "new way from Alberta." Jack was flying the flag of the Alberta Prophet on a pole by his house. Jack had recently come out of the hospital and the Alberta Prophet had instructed him, it was said, to fly the flag to assure recovery and continuing health. For the treaty feast and festivities in late June of that year, Jack was the chief's *k'awo*. A *k'awo* is a boss consensually chosen to organize a group enterprise (see appendix). Lurie and I helped Jack gain access to the community hall for the dances following treaty payment[5] and had, through Vital as interpreter, a friendly and animated exchange. Jack was much in evidence organizing and arranging the 1967 treaty festivities, and we were immediately intrigued by him as a personality. He had an intense manner and piercing gaze when serious, but he also displayed an engaging grin and sense of fun. In our field notes Lurie described him as merry. At the dance Jack as *k'awo* provoked general hilarity as he went about playfully striking young men with a switch and swatting some older women on the rump to get them on the dance floor. This was the month before Jack made his second visit to the Alberta Prophet and returned as a prophet in his own right.

In November 1967, when Lurie and I returned for the month, the change in Jack's persona was striking. Gone was the merry demeanor; all was solemnity. We immediately heard a complaint that Jack had "spoiled the fun" following a wedding. He kept the dances short and limited to his "sacred" drum songs; it was apparently impossible to get the more popular (and secular) tea dance started. On a number of fronts Jack continued to put himself at odds with some people's expectations and values. For the Easter feast and dances in 1968 the Old Chief replaced

Dog team on the new ice of Marian Lake soon after freezeup. Rae, November, 1967.

Jack with another *k'awo*. The explanation was that the Old Chief and
other consequential men had been affronted by Jack's breach of protocol
in not "telling the chief what he had been doing." Specifically, he had not
paid the customary visit and report to the chief upon his return from the
dog team trip he had just led to visit Naidzo in Fort Franklin. To older
Dogribs, the Old Chief was the symbol of Dogrib unity—"that old man
is like our flag"—and responsible men were supposed to apprise the chief
of their travels and information gained. At treaty time in the summer of
1968 Jack appeared at the treaty feast to announce that he would not join
in. His position was that he had worked well when he was *k'awo* and he
should have at least have been asked to help. But since he had not been,
he would not join in the feast. Vital attributed Jack's refusal to his being
"jealous because he's no longer *k'awo.*" But Barthelemy, speaking at the
feast, lamented, "The poor Prophet has just left us; that doesn't look
good."[6] In the same week the Chief's incumbent *k'awo* reported that Jack
had urged him to confiscate all playing cards in town, which the *k'awo*
refused to do. By this time there was also an accusation circulating that
Jack had "stolen some of the feast money" when he was treaty *k'awo* in
June of the previous year.

For Jack the contrast between his ascendancy as prophet and cult leader
and his relegation to being an ordinary citizen in the community-wide
events of treaty time must have been galling. Only the previous Sunday

he had dominated a large crowd as impresario and star performer at the prophet dance at Marian River. His annunciation of prophetic authority had already taken on an autocratic cast. At an earlier public gathering, he had announced, "If you don't believe me, you're going to go to hell." People were commenting that some of his adherents were kneeling before him while signing the cross and calling him *Gota* ('Our Father'). That he was presenting himself, or permitting others to treat him as, a quasi-divinity was, for some, outré at the least.

To Vital, Jack's grandstanding and domineering behavior, so out of line with Dogrib social proprieties, was nothing new. "He always was a big talker. Even when he was thirteen or fourteen, he would tell a group of men, 'Let me talk, this is the way it happened.' Now he can talk all he wants!" In that summer of 1968 persons disinclined to believe in Jack's authenticity as a prophet were commenting that it was hard to believe in a prophet who had long been a womanizer. Accusations included an account that he had once gone to jail for getting a twelve-year-old girl pregnant. These persons did not seem to consider the possibility of a reformed rake. By the next summer (1969) word was about that Jack was announcing that it was all right to go after any woman and to trade wives because that is what women are for. A story also was circulating that the Marten Lake Dogribs were angry because while visiting there Jack had had intercourse with one of the local girls. In light of the accusatory gossip, it is not surprising that Jack was reported as saying that there are only three sins—drinking, card playing, and talking about people behind their backs. It was people talking behind his back, Jack announced, that had made him "pure and white like the snow," and he traveled to heaven like that. (In cultural fact, to talk behind another's back is an infringement on the deeply-held Dene social value of respect for the autonomy of the individual, the right of everyone to be his own boss [Helm 1961:173-76]. See Naidzo's stricture against talking about Jack, below. Rushforth [1981:35-37] provides, in respect the Bearlake Indians specifically, a rich discussion of that value.)

Jack continued to show disrespect for the Old Chief by not reporting to him on trips taken. And, as treaty time approached in 1969, the Old Chief and others resented that Jack was holding his followers at a distance from Rae until the actual day of treaty payment. By Vital's account, the Old Chief said, "It's no more like before. This guy [Jack] is spoiling everything. Indians used to all come in [to Rae] from the spring hunt and everybody is glad to meet. Now they [Jack's followers] stay on the island, dancing and preaching." Jack's drive to organize and direct, a quality useful in a chief's *k'awo*, now was not serving the community as a whole.

Rather, he was interposing a kind of sectarian opposition to social accord and solidarity.

By Christmas 1969 an intriguing explanation of the source of Jack's prophecy had emerged: "His *ink'on* is fooling him." This seemed to be not an accusation that Jack was consciously drawing on his *ink'on*, but rather that Jack himself was unaware of the invalid force directing his prophecy. A few months later a story circulated which, if true, indicates that Jack was experiencing mental stress or emotional perturbation: he had twice been seen standing outside naked.

By 1976, Jack's activities as a prophet were essentially over. In that year, one of the priests at Rae described him as having been very depressed for a period but now "coming up again." Now Jack was active in the N.W.T. Indian Brotherhood (later, the Dene Nation), campaigning in support of the successful candidate for its presidency and promulgating its opposition to a projected gas pipeline through the Northwest Territories (Berger 1977; Helm 1980). In addition, through the local priest's influence he had been appointed "craft instructor," a position that actually involved running a bush school for boys and teenagers, at the new day school built for the Dogrib children of Rae.[7] In the priest's judgment Jack's significant role was as a communicator of Dogrib knowledge and values, holding his young audience rapt by the hour. His drive for influence and authority had found new outlets.

3

The Foundations of Prophecy

Society, Authority, and the Prophets

Dogrib society held no monolithic public opinion with respect to the three prophets or any one of them. Even among Dogribs of the same sex and age group who shared broadly similar life experiences, individuals' responses to the prophets were affected by distinctive casts of mind, biases, and perspectives. (For Vital, Barthelemy had long been a respected community leader and friend, yet Vital emphatically and overtly parted with Barthelemy on the question of Jack's legitimacy as a prophet.) Nonetheless, as news and gossip circulated, quasi-collective judgments formed and were reinforced as individuals "listened to" one another's opinions about the prophets. (Roberts notes, "The normal gossip of any group is actually a slow scanning of the total informational resource of the group" [1964:441].) Some aspects of the relationships, reactions, and judgments of Dogribs in respect to the prophets have emerged in prior sections. As those aspects exemplify more broadly shared opinions, they bear on the salience of the prophets, singly and together, from 1967 to 1971, when they commanded the greatest attention from the Dogrib community.

The salience of the prophets was rooted in the contexture of authority. As used here, authority is the quality of *rightly* commanding assent and allegiance. Persons and groups, statuses and institutions have authority insofar as individuals and collectivities of individuals acknowledge them to be endued with that quality. The authority of the prophets flows from their authenticity: their visions and messages must be deemed true. In the case of each prophet, the truth of his prophecy is composed of a double strand—that the revelatory experience is real and that the source of the experience is valid. The speculation that "Jack's *ink'on* is fooling him" proposed that the source of his prophecy was invalid. To accept a prophet as true, a Dogrib of the 1960s must believe that a person can experience or enter into the state of being *nate* (a 'dreamer', a 'prophet'), and that the source that informs the person's prophecy is God—as his intent is disclosed through his supramundane representants and emissaries as the prophet encounters those beings in heaven or on earth.[1] The reality of those beings and the prophet's experiences is verified by the postulates of the individual Dogrib's "culturally constituted belief system" (Spiro 1966:101). The prophet's legitimacy comes from the ultimate authority of the God who invests the Roman Catholic Church and its priests with their authority.

Judgments concerning the prophets rendered by persons holding three sorts of authority statuses in Dogrib society carried special import with respect to the prophets' authenticity and importance. The local priests were the arbiters of the church's authority over morals and religious belief. The prophets themselves constituted special authorities with respect to the validity of others' prophecies. In addition, a partial congelation of quasi-public authority was constituted by the loosely bounded set of middle-aged and elderly men whose "advice and consent" buttressed the stature of the Old Chief as the singular personage embodying the diffuse authority of the Dogrib communality over its members.

The socially authoritative core of judgment and decision making in Dogrib society and polity was lodged in these older men. This is not to say that outside that ambit the reactions and opinions of other adult Dogribs—women and younger men—respecting the prophecies of Naidzo, Chi, and Jack did not feed into the ongoing society-wide evaluative processes. Women attended prophets' sessions as they did other public events such as feasts and dances. Many women accepted the authenticity of the prophets or at the least appreciated their influence in stemming alcohol abuse. Women's influence on issues and public opinion, however, was limited to familial and personal networks. Women held no special statuses or "offices," traditional or otherwise. When consequential men came together to discuss political and public issues, no women (other than, on rare occasions, myself) were present. Neither were young men. Certainly information and opinions filtered between the male generations through casual interaction and conversation. But when men in Rae were called to the Old Chief's house for a parley on matters of public policy and polity, almost no one under the age of forty was present or was expected to be. Conspicuously absent were those several school-educated young men in their twenties who were active in the pan-Dene movement emerging in the 1960s. One of these was Barthelemy's son.

In earlier pages, I estimated that in the Rae-Yellowknife interaction sphere the "adult" audience (those aged twenty or older) for the prophets was at most about 770 persons, male and female. Of those, only about 200 men were over forty (see table 1). These were the men who, "listening to one another," were in both the traditional view and their own the significant judgmental authorities on public matters in Dogrib society.

Out of these 200 men who had known one another for a lifetime, those whose qualities of character and engagement in social and political issues lent special weight to their opinions were perhaps one-third that number. (That is not to say that one-third of them regularly interacted or were available in Rae.) Generally included in this cadre were those whose capabilities had been recognized at one time or another by consensual selection for leadership roles, especially those men who had filled more ongoing roles such as regional band leader-"councillor" and, preeminently, the Old Chief, prime leader for more than thirty years (see appendix).

With his repertoire of Dogrib history and legend, Naidzo reanimated the people's past as the older generations had lived it or learned it from their elders. Those auditors aged sixty-five or more could themselves recall the harsh virtues of Dogrib life before the highway, before automobiles or even outboard motors, before schools and welfare and medical services, before liquor or even brew, before Treaty—when all lived in the bush year round and gained and shared life's sustenance from it. The older people were aware that the generation-cum-culture gap was fast widening between them and many of the young people, threatening a crisis for the traditional authority of elders. Vital, speaking to his peers at a meeting at the Old Chief's house in the early 1960s, said, "All these young fellows are just like they are lost. They won't listen to one another [i.e., join in the consensual community]. That's what spoils the whole band [Dogrib society]" (translation from tape). As divinely inspired authorities, the prophets buttressed the moral and social authority of their peers, the mature and elderly, in the face of the accelerating changes of the 1960s.

Naidzo and Jack excited greater and more sustained attention from the general body of adults and from the consequential men than did Chi. Chi's reclusive isolation at Marten Lake and probably his particular prophetic persona constricted his impact. Individuals might not take Chi's or Naidzo's messages to heart and practice, but those prophets' behavioral styles were exemplary by Dogrib standards. They presented themselves

Relaxing after the treaty feast. Rae, 1962.

as part of the ideally consensual community, fully in accord with accepted modes of authority and respectful of the autonomy of others, seeking simply to preach, to persuade others to heed the divine authority that informed their prophecies.

Jack was another matter. The rituals per se of the Alberta prophet cult that Jack introduced brought no sense of threat or offense to traditional belief or observance, Roman Catholic or otherwise (at least, I heard no complaints). Jack's personal style of behavior was the problem. He repeatedly flouted the authority of the Old Chief by not reporting to him after his extended travels. He tried to boss the Old Chief's incumbent *k'awo* by demanding that the latter confiscate all playing cards in the community. He breached Dogrib solidarity by keeping his *et'at'in* followers in cultic observances at a distance from Rae instead of joining the ingathering of the outlying band-communities as treaty time approached. Everyone knew, including the Old Chief himself, that the Old Chief must soon step down due to his advanced deafness. In the opinion of some, Jack wanted to be the next head chief. (Vital opined, "I think those *et'at'in* are pushing Jack from behind, the way he's talking.") The apprehension that Jack was undermining the ideal of Dogrib communality and mutual respect appeared to underlie many of the more specifically phrased objections to his behavior.

As prophetic authorities, the three Dogrib prophets evinced distinctive responses to others' prophecies. By taking on the ritual complex of the Alberta cult, Jack demonstrated that he subscribed to the validity of the Alberta prophets and to the authority of the main prophet but thereby raised the question of his own authenticity (see Naidzo's comment below). While promulgating and extending his own prophecy, Jack sought out Naidzo at Fort Franklin as a fellow prophet. News of the Bear Lake Prophet that Jack and his fellow visitors to Franklin brought back to Rae was apparently the catalyst that launched Naidzo's career at Rae. Whether Jack ever questioned any aspect of Naidzo's or Chi's prophetic authority I have no evidence. Chi's one-time visit to Rae, at Christmas 1969, did not provide much opportunity for most Dogribs to hear his views of the other prophets. According to Vital, Chi "didn't like" Jack talking so much about Jesus at the Christmas feast. Chi's statement that he saw no ribbons on the drums in heaven implied a challenge to the authenticity of Jack's account of the drums in heaven.

Naidzo had found the Alberta Prophet's style of "scolding" his auditors distasteful. And, according to Vital, he had some doubt as to Jack's authenticity: "It's hard to say. Maybe Jack won't last long. But don't tell him, because it is not nice to talk behind the back of person who talks about God. But Jack carries another person's story [i.e., the Alberta Prophet's]." (Here the intimation is that a prophet's "truth" arises only from the prophet's own visionary experience; this point is addressed later). Naidzo's endorsement of Chi, however, was unqualified. "Listen to Chi," he is reported to have said. "We have both seen the same thing, four drums in heaven [an oblique reference to Jack having seen *seven* drums with *ribbons*] and the wings for the people. . . . Chi has seen it all [the same things that Naidzo saw in heaven] and I never told him about it."

The local priests were important, indeed pivotal, authorities with respect to the validity of the prophets. The Roman Catholic Church, represented by priests of the order of Oblates of Immaculate Mary *(les Missionaries oblates de Marie immaculée),* is the one institution of the Euro-Canadian world that has been incorporated into the indigenous authority system of the Dogrib people.

The first Oblate entered Dogrib country in 1859. The prior year marked the advent of Christian (Roman Catholic and Anglican) proselytization in the Mackenzie region. Within twenty years or so, the bulk of the Dene had been baptized in the Roman Catholic faith. Anglican misssionaries, less quick to baptize, made converts among other linguistic-tribal divisions of the Dene but not among the Dogribs. According to an Oblate historian, "The [Oblate] missionaries do not hesitate to regard the Dogribs, in spite of their conspicuous faults, as the best Catholics of the Mackenzie. . . . All the campaigns organized by the [Anglican] heresy have failed completely at Fort Rae" (Duchaussois 1928:303, my translation). Frank Russell, who in 1894 traveled for two months with a Dogrib band, remarked that the "Dog Ribs are very strict in the observance of the outward forms of the Catholic Church," saying grace in concert before all meals, holding Sunday services, and, when traveling, saying prayers before commencing each day's journey. "They displayed heroic faith when they knelt in the snows of the Barren Ground to offer up prayers with chattering teeth, shifting their rosaries with half frozen fingers" (1898:162).

Throughout the Mackenzie region the Oblate fathers stand apart from other whites in respect to their integration into the society of their Dene congregations. Coming commonly from France, the Oblates spend their lives in daily interaction with their Dene parishioners, remaining for many years at one mission and being the only whites who speak an Athapaskan language. The other whites resident in the North, many of whom are there as agents of some part of government, are usually Protestant, often transient, and, even if sympathetically inclined, have but superficial interaction with or knowledge of the Dene peoples.

Some of the younger Dogribs, especially the school-educated bicultural youths, might view the church and its Oblate priests as old-fashioned, authoritarian, and repressive of the right of individuals to make free choices of lifestyle.[2] But I think it correct to say that the great majority of Dogribs of the 1960s believed church dogma as received through instruction by the Oblates and accepted the priests as authorities in religious matters. All the older generations may not have been as devout communicants of the church as Barthelemy, but even to those less engaged the Roman Catholic church was their church, and its priests their priests.

St. Michael's Mission (now Parish), which also serves all outlying Dogrib hamlets attached to Rae, had two resident Oblates. In the 1960s and '70s they encouraged and aided Dogribs, mostly older men, to attend the intertribal religious assemblies in southern Alberta, at the Catholic shrine of Ste. Anne (where Barthelemy learned of the Alberta Prophet) and at the yearly ecumenical congresses of Indians at Morley, where Indians from tribes in Canada and the United States sought traditional as well as contemporary routes to spiritual enlightenment (Stanley 1977).[3]

To the two priests serving at Rae, the three Dogrib prophets' preachments constituted no crisis of religious authority. The priests could

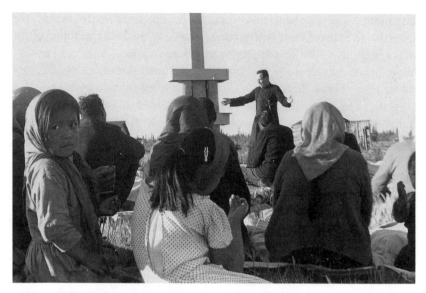

Oblate priest preaching at the cross erected at Lac la Martre. 1960.

only welcome the prophets' attacks on drinking and their exhortations to reflect on one's spiritual condition and to pray to God for help and guidance. Chi's impact as a prophet was in any case apparently circumscribed. Naidzo received unstinting support from the clergy. The esteem and respect expressed by a priest at Great Bear Lake—"Naidzo is a fine Christian gentlemen"—was echoed by the Oblate fathers at Rae. "Naidzo was truly holy, a great man," was one's assessment after Naidzo's death. At a mundane level, the priests of the Rae mission aided in collecting money to pay for Naidzo's plane trips to Rae and were the medium by which news of his visits was quickly relayed by radio "sched" to the outlying Dogrib communities.

Excessive and obsessive aspects of Jack's prophetic style met with strictures from the local Oblates. In the spring of 1968, following Jack's assumption of prophecy the previous summer, a letter from a middle-aged Dogrib reported, "Jack used to dance everyday holding the rosary and he used to make the sign of the cross every minute, but he doesn't do that anymore since Father told him not to do that. So now he dances just once every two weeks and no more holding the rosary when dancing." (Actually, dancing with rosary continued.) Later comments of other Dogribs also indicated that the priests exerted their authority in an effort to damp Jack's more obsessive religiosity. That some of his adherents knelt before him and addressed him as Our Father was (expectably) one point at issue. On the whole, however, the priests' control was muted, too much so for some Dogribs offended by what they saw as Jack's excesses. On several occasions, one of the local priests, as he informed me in a later year, turned the pulpit over to Jack, though he had to caution him to brush the angels (that hovered about Jack as he preached) off his shoulders. It was clear that the aim of the Oblate fathers at Rae was not to reject Jack or turn the community against him (though one priest allowed himself a muttered aside about "prophets and profiteers") but to nurture his spiritual development in the longer run. By 1976, when Jack had abandoned his public role as prophet to turn his moral and intellectual energies to working with the youth and for the Indian Brotherhood, one priest judged, "Give him ten or twenty years, he'll be a great man."

Qualities of Dogrib Prophecy

The intent of the messages of the three Dogrib prophets was the same, to frame, as Wallace describes the code of the Iroquois prophet Handsome Lake, "a chart of conduct by which a man may live honorably in this world and happily in the next" (1966:8). The lure of and reward for honorable living is that happy next world, the Christian's heaven: in Naidzo's joyous vision, a vast and shining "playground" where one's wings wait and food materializes at the thought. The well-lived life is in the service of one's soul, the means to attain heaven. The manifest content of each prophet's message merged with how the prophet delivered his message, the timbre of prophetic performance and persona, to create the three distinctive styles of prophecy examined in prior pages.

For those who accepted the prophecy of Jack, Naidzo, or Chi, the prophet was a holy man, a divinely inspired preacher. The ritual of the prophet dance placed Jack also in the role of cult leader. His effort to establish a congregation of prophet-acolytes and followers contrasted with the performance modes of Chi and Naidzo. As divinely inspired teachers, Naidzo and Chi offered spiritual succor and salvation to those who heeded their words. Jack presented as well rites beyond Church liturgy as part of the road to spiritual knowledge and salvation. Neither Naidzo nor Chi enjoined ritual enactments upon those who would follow their teachings. This common "negative" trait aside, in prophetic persona and performance Naidzo and Chi departed pronouncedly from one another. Naidzo was extroverted and expansive, incorporating entertainments in the course of his prophet performance—legends, lore, jokes, teasing flirtation. In contrast to Chi's vision of the horrors attending drinking and card playing, Naidzo affirmatively encouraged rather than frightened his auditors to observe his teachings with respect to good conduct. Naidzo's ebullient and confident self-presentation contrasted with the anxious affectivity of Chi and the imperious and obsessive style of Jack.

Handelman has observed that "the shaman as actor of a social role performing according to the requisites of the sociocultural unit . . . has effectively obscured the possible range of variation of personality among shamans, and usually only the overt portion of the shamanic iceberg, visual and explicitly behavioral, is treated by anthropologists" (1968:353). Applying that admonition to the prophetic iceberg, even on the "visual and explicitly behavioral level," the three Dogrib prophets-as-actors come across as having three kinds of temperaments and characters. They certainly do not add up to a Dogrib "prophetic personality" type. And with respect to the "requisites of the sociocultural unit"—the unit here being the Dogrib people of the late 1960s— apparently the social-behavioral style of the prophet-actor loomed larger than the form of the prophetic performance. As noted, among those inclined to be seriously interested in the validity and import of prophecies, disbelief by some of them in Jack's prophecy was phrased variously in terms of his suspect moral character, his imperious behavior, and his *ink'on* as a false source of inspiration, rather than rejection of rites of the prophet dance as such.

If there is no Dogrib prophetic personality type, is there a Dogrib cultural form or style of prophecy? The question opens some avenues of exploration of the cultural-conceptional underpinnings of Dogrib prophecy. Certainly Dogrib prophetic form and performance is embedded in broader Northern Dene comprehensions that are in turn enmeshed in the historical processes of intercultural contacts and borrowings from beyond the Dene realm. It is not the purpose of this study to venture a panoramic foray into Dene culture history and process. Rather, proceeding from Dogrib comprehensions, it is to explore what constitutes prophecy. Here evidence respecting Dogrib memories of other prophets is germane.

Earlier Prophets

Naidzo, Chi, and Jack were not the first prophets or persons purporting to be prophets known to living Dogribs. Embedded in field notes from 1959 into the 1970s are statements about several earlier prophets. I present these prophets in roughly chronological order. Information gained in the field is followed by supporting documentary evidence, when available.

The earliest remembered prophets. In November 1967, while Vital and I were discussing the Roman Catholic mission and its history, Vital recounted the story of the first missionary to travel to the Rae Lakes *et'at'in* country. History identifies him as the Oblate priest Emile Petitot and the year as 1864.

> The first priest that came to the Old Fort [i.e., Fort Rae at its first location at Mountain Island, some miles from the present Rae] was called *Yahtigon.* That means "Skinny Father" or "Tall Father." Some Indians never knew Father came in. Father came in late fall—no, in winter [actually, in spring]. Father had two guides [confirmed by Petitot]. He made a trip way down to where Andrew Gon's camp is now [at Rae Lakes, in *et'at'in* country]. That is the first place where a Father ever met Indians [i.e., Dogribs; actually, the first Oblate contact with Dogribs was at Old Fort Rae in 1859.] It was a big camp. There were so many prophets then, before the priests. And they had an argument with that first priest. Some guys had two or three wives and Father said that was no good. They didn't understand one another much, but Father had an interpreter. [Petitot speaks only of "guides," but I suspect Vital is correct, given Petitot's use of the Chipewyan dialect for native terms]. I don't know how long Father stayed but some of the Indians treated him good. But other Indians didn't believe him because they already had a prophet. That prophet was like a priest. After Father left, the prophets all died.

In July of 1969, Vital gave a variant account:

> There used to be prophets before the priest, that's what they say. The *et'at'in* had some.[4] The Father got mad. The first priest that visited the Indian camps was talking about God and prayer. There were two *et'at'in* prophets. [Petitot says four.] When the priest was talking about God and prayer and so forth, the prophets said "we know that" and started to preach alongside the priest—like Jack. All the Indians believed in the prophets, so the priest got few people. Father said, "That's not right. I came here to talk about God, bible history, and pray. These two prophets don't know much." Sometime afterward there was a flu that cleaned [killed] the prophets. At Rae Lakes there is a [former] village, *komorela,* a name that means

something like a graveyard. That's because so many died in that village.

Vital's knowledge of the confrontation of the priest and the "prophets" cannot be assumed to stem solely from Dogrib oral tradition, for it is likely that successions of Oblate priests at the Rae mission have expatiated on this event through the years. Petitot (1865, 1891) wrote at least two full accounts of the incident, which occurred at an encampment of 600 (by his estimate; 1891:219) Dogribs in the Rae Lakes region. Petitot's first narrative, written as a report to his superior in 1864 on the events in May of that year, is the more immediate account and I follow it here. Petitot prefaced his report of the confrontation with the "prophets" by stressing that

> the tribe [the assemblage at Rae Lakes] is greatly disposed to *inkanse [ink'on;* Petitot used the Chipewyan word rather than the Dogrib] or superstitious medicine: I have counted almost 60 *jongleurs* [in the encampment]. . . . Everything shown to them through dream is considered as true. It is often through dream that they make what they call medicine, a ridiculous practice to which they attach the cure of diseases, the success of undertakings, the death of a person. For a long time, they thought that the [Catholic] priest, like *jongleurs,* only taught the wild imaginings of his mind. [Petitot 1865:382]

Petitot had been in the encampment over a week, baptizing children and instructing in the faith, before the confrontation developed.

> Now four[5] of these *jongleurs*-dreamers had imagined one night that God had transformed them into priests; there they are showing themselves to the public and pretending to be inspired. They promise the savages three kinds of heaven, a black, a grey, and a white one, and this according to their degree of holiness; they announce that from now on they would have nothing to do with Christian priests because mass, confession, the sacraments, all this is useless. One of them invents a song that he says has been dictated by God himself, and this burlesque song very soon becomes popular in the tribe. No one before I arrived had dared contradict the imposters. Their lies were effective and the savages submitted to their direction. Fortunately God has allowed that those religion makers do not talk against baptism; on the contrary, they wanted it for themselves and for their children; and this was enough to demonstrate to the men of good sense that the *jongleurs* were

Danites Flancs-de-Chien. (Lac des Pyrites, Klé-ri-tʒié.)

A few days after his confrontation with the Dogrib *jongleurs,* Petitot sketched these Dogribs in their lodge at the time he erected a wooden cross (13 May 1868) at "Lac des Pyrites" and renamed it Lac St. Croix. Engraving in Petitot (1891:286); photographic reproduction courtesy of the Smithsonian Institution.

something completely different from the priests.

One Sunday, after having celebrated high mass and baptized some fifteen adults, I was having my lunch when someone came to announce that the four prophets *[prophètes]* were holding a meeting on the next hill. I take myself there; I find there most of the tribe. The savages were seated, their legs crossed, in front of a large lodge where the four squatting charlatans were singing at the top of their lungs the song they had invented. I clap my hands to impose silence. Then I reproach the crowd for scorning my word and for the evil it commits by following the counsels of some hallucinators. [Petitot 1865:383; translation by June Helm and Bella Bouaziz; shifts in tense are Petitot's.]

Petitot continues with an account of his exchange with one of the *jongleur*-prophets, who shouted, "Who are you to come and disturb us? . . . You don't see God! Well, I see him and I can talk to him face-to-face . . ."[6] The end result was that Petitot threatened to leave, "the savages apologized profusely," and the "chiefs" begged Petitot not to abandon them. Petitot conceded that he would stay a while longer to instruct the people and baptize some of them, but there would be no baptism that year for the *jongleurs* (Petitot 1865:384-85).

In his writings about the incident Petitot bestows several labels upon the four "charlatans": *jongleurs, jongleurs-rêveurs, prophètes, clairvoyants* (1865:383, 384); also *illuminés, chamans du bon Dieu,* and *voyants et prêtres de Niolsti* [Christian God] (1891:223, 224). *Jongleur* he elsewhere equates with *chaman, prétendu magicien sauvage,* and for the Hare dialect specifies *nate, 'rêveur',* as the Athapaskan equivalent (1876:224). The *jongleurs'* claim that they had spoken directly with God doubtlessly led Petitot to assign them the label, even if ironic, of prophets and accounts for Vital's designation in English. In the present day the term *nate* 'dreamer', specifies a prophet, such as Naidzo, to the Dogribs rather than (just?) an *ink'on* adept.

The Snare Prophet. A Dogrib described the Snare Prophet (my designation) as "a holy man, an Indian who prayed for everyone like the Fathers." He is buried in an old graveyard in the Snare River–Snare Lake region where the *detcinlahot'in,* the Edge-of-the-Woods regional band, interred their dead in years past. From a tree in the graveyard hangs the white cup of the prophet with "letters" on it that change every year. The prophet's great grandson, his last direct descendant in the male line, who bore the English surname Prophet, drowned with a companion while on the fall caribou hunt along the Snare River route in 1964. Estimating twenty-five- to thirty-year intervals between the birth of the Snare Prophet, his son, his grandson, and his great-grandson in 1919, the prophet was perhaps born between 1830 and 1845. That span of dates accords with Vital's understanding that he was an "old, old timer," who was an adult "before the [first] priest came" in the 1860s.

On the fall caribou hunt of 1959, one of the Oblate priests at Rae accompanied those hunters taking the Snare River–Snare Lake route toward the hunting grounds. He described the Snare Prophet as a holy man, buried in the graveyard that the Edge-of-the-Woods people had asked him to consecrate on Assumption Sunday. "Maybe this year," said a Dogrib at Rae on that Sunday, calculating that the hunters were now at the burial site, "they will be able to read the letters on the cup."

To Vital, the proof of the Snare Prophet's authenticity was that before the priests came he knew about the cross. "He used to make a cross with sticks. God knows how he finds out, because before the priest nobody knows about the cross. After the Father came with the cross, he said, 'The old man must be true'. The prophet was still alive when the priest came." Vital recalled another story about the Snare Prophet that he had heard as a boy:

One time, I don't know if it was before or after the priest came, all the men from a big camp went to hunt musk ox [this suggests a time frame between 1875 and 1900]. But the prophet was too old, so he stayed behind. There were no men in the camp, just women and the old prophet. In the morning it was Easter Day and he invited everyone to come to his place. "We will say our prayers and have a good feed, because this is a big day, a holiday because Jesus came alive. Even the sun is so happy that the sun dances. That means that everybody must be happy today, so we will eat and have a dance." And all the Indians [the women] believed him and they danced pretty near all day. That is the story I heard. I think the old prophet was right [true].

Ayha. Ayha (Ayah, Ereya) was one of the Dogribs attached to Fort Franklin (probably as a result of the departure of the Bear Lake Chief's band from Rae in 1914) and is buried there. Judging from the age of a son born in 1901—that son being recognized by local priests as a "medicine man" who cured a mentally ill girl at Marten Lake after he moved back to Rae in his old age—Ayha probably was born between 1860 and 1880. A middle-aged woman recalled that when she was about fourteen (about 1933), "at Christmas we heard that a prophet from Franklin came to Hottah Lake [at the farthest reach of the *et'at'in* range] and all the people from Marian Lake [part of the *et'at'in*] went to Hottah Lake. We mixed with the Franklin people and stayed until Easter. There was a big feast and dance and lots of caribou." The prophet was surely Ayha. An Oblate priest who had been stationed for some years at Fort Franklin described Ayha as "the great prophet of the Dogribs' history. When alive he had much more influence and a more lasting one than Jack or Naidzo. He could foresee the future and knew what happened in his absence."[7]

Harry Natéa. One of Jack's prophet songs was attributed to Harry Natéa. According to Vital, Naidzo said, "I think Harry was true." An aged Dogrib (b. 1888) from Dettah recalled that a few years after Treaty (1921) there was a prophet at Fort Providence, a Slavey, a really good prophet whose song "we still sing today." This was probably Harry Natéa. By Vital's recollection, Harry died not long after the great influenza epidemic of 1928.

The ethnologist Osgood reported that in the winter of 1925–26, three years before his fieldwork in the region, "a new religious cult" reached Great Bear Lake by way of the Marten Lake Dogribs from the Rae Dogribs, in response to the rise of a "Messiah" at Providence. From the time period and Naidzo's familiarity with Harry Natéa, it seems likely that Harry was Osgood's "Messiah."

> A message was sent by the [Rae] chief [this would have been Monhwi, the Old Chief's predecessor] to the Bear Lake Chief [the Dogrib leader of Naidzo's band] apprising him of the importance of the new cult and he has acted since as its leader in that vicinity. The cult activity is principally a dance. Before starting the ceremony, everyone must wash and dress his hair. Both men and women dance in a single circle to the accompaniment of a beaten drum before which each of the dancers bows in passing.
>
> The cult is supposed to have originated with a man of supernatural power who lived at Providence on the upper Mackenzie river. When one of the Indians was ill with an epileptic fit, this shaman was called in. He thereupon hit the ground with his stick and told the man to rise, which he immediately did, completely cured. So great did his fame become for this and other deeds that he was called a "Messiah" [prophet?]. How the ceremony became part of the cult, no one seemed to know.
>
> The "Messiah Cult" is widespread among the Indians but it may be only of temporary significance, especially since so much sickness and death have appeared concurrently. [Osgood 1932:87. Osgood was in the field in 1928, the year of the great influenza epidemic.]

A rejected prophet. Vital recalled that in years past Joseph Marrow (b. 1881) had claimed to be a prophet. He tried to "teach" the people and to sing. But people decided he was "talking mostly about his *ink'on*, so they left him and he quit." Joseph died in the early 1960s. (Joseph was the last specific case of prophecy I extracted from Vital. When I asked if there had been others as well, Vital replied, "Oh, lots—but they didn't last long.")[8]

Components of Prophecy

The several prophecies of present and past parse into four components: revelation, moral teaching or the preaching of a code of conduct, inspired song, and (in two cases) ritual. Except for the ritual observances imported by Jack, only in Osgood's report on the Providence (Slavey) Messiah is there found among the Dogrib ritual (involving dance and song) imposed by a prophet. If the Providence Messiah was indeed Harry Natéa, apparently the ritualistic component of his prophecy has been lost to memory or is now deemed inconsequential. Group ritual seems to be an adventitious component of Dogrib prophecy. In fact, the only "complex, stereotyped sequences that we . . . call rituals" known in Dogrib cultural history have been those introduced as components of the "ecclesiastical cult institution" (Wallace 1966:68, 87–88) of the Roman Catholic Church. The southerly Dene sources of the rituals of Jack and the Providence Messiah argue for the strong possibility of transmissions of stereotypic cultic enactments through intertribal contacts from beyond the Dene culture area, where ritual has been more manifest, to the Dene populations, now classified as Beaver and Slavey, exploiting the drainages of the Peace, Hay, and Fort Nelson rivers.[9]

The prophet's own inspired song seems to be regarded as an integral feature of true prophecy. Only in the case of Ayha is evidence of a prophet song lacking. Harry Natéa's song was borrowed by Jack along with, so Dogribs said, songs from the Alberta prophets, thereby raising questions about Jack's authenticity. Chi's inspired songs of "heaven people" lent validity to his prophecy. Naidzo, strangely, revealed his songs only in the last months of his life. Joseph Marrow (a pseudonym), the rejected prophet, had a song, and the song of one of Petitot's *jongleurs* "that he says has been dictated by God himself" was part of the prophetic claim of those Rae Lakes prophets. That the Snare Prophet called upon the women of the camp to dance indicates song, of course, for song is the accompaniment of dance for the Dogribs, but we are not told that it was a "holy" song composed or received by the prophet.[10] To the present day, group dance celebrates the coming together of the people in joy and amity. It is by no means religious ritualism.

As with Jack, Naidzo, and Chi, past prophets came to their prophecies through revealed knowledge of and experience in the Christian supernal world. This is inferred in the case of Ayha and Harry Natéa: Natéa's song was about "heaven people," and the priest's assessment of Ayha's influence as "the great prophet of Dogrib's history" presupposes Christian divine guidance. (That Ayha foretold events is not a characteristic attributed to the other prophets in Dogribs' accounts; it is apparently as adventitious as ritual.) As a teacher imparting an inspired message, Ayha's role parallels those of the three present Dogrib prophets. That the Snare Prophet is viewed as a a holy man suggests a similar role. Petitot provides no sense of what might have constituted the "holiness" of which one of his four *jongleurs* spoke. Petitot denied its validity in any case. That known Dogrib prophecies derive from the imperatives of the supreme Christian deity raises the knotty question—far beyond the scope of this study—of what Dene prophecy was before God. Certainly revelation and preaching are at the heart of Dogrib prophecy as living generations have known it.

Prophecy and Ink'on

The prophet's song expressing the divine revelation suggests a point of correspondence, indeed a cultural homology, with the revelatory experience of the person who gains *ink'on*. On the other hand, certain qualities of prophecy and of *ink'on* potency are, analytically, contrastive. The nature of prophecy and its core attributes of revelation and preaching as understood by Dogribs come into sharper focus through comparison with *ink'on*.

In a discussion of medicine power among the Chipewyan Dene, David M. Smith stresses the essential monism of Chipewyan thought, wherein seeming categorical distinctions are those of "polarity (extremes of the same dimension) and not of . . . true opposition (as between entities or conditions that exclude or deny one another)" (1988). That point bears on *ink'on* and prophecy among the Dogrib. In the present-day Dogrib conceptions as revealed by native statements, prophecy and *ink'on* are not in opposition as "good" versus "evil" or "true" versus "false." In acceptable practice, however, they compose a contrariety, or reciprocal exclusion. As imputed by Dogribs in the cases of Jack and Joseph Marrow, *ink'on* is not false as a potency; it is false only as a source of Christian prophecy. Further, Naidzo's account of his path to prophecy suggests that Dene *ink'on* and Christian prophecy are antipathetic. The first step in bringing Naidzo to prophecy was to "clean out" all his *ink'on*. And Chi ceased the practice of *ink'on* curing before he assumed his prophecy.

Dogrib communicants of the Roman Catholic faith, such as Vital, accept *ink'on* as a reality that exists on another track or dimension from the reality of the heaven, divine personages, and mysteries circumscribed by the dogma of the Roman Catholic Church. The absolutism of Euro-Christian authority which must hold *ink'on*—ipso facto gained through communication with non-Christian "individuated animate agencies," to borrow Brightman's phrasing (1988:366)—to be false or a manifestation of satanic forces has not imprinted on Dene comprehensions of the dimensions of valid experience.[11]

Where *ink'on* and prophecy merge apperceptively is in the "truth" (validity) of personal, individual *experience* with other-than-human beings—experience that authorizes the prophet and potentiates the *ink'on*-endowed to shape the course of events. Treating of "ways of knowing with the mind" among the Dene of northern Alberta, from whom Jack borrowed his prophet ceremony, Goulet (1990) stresses the primacy of individual experience in Dene traditional religion, that religion is predominantly experiential, that a person with religious experience is described not as a believer but as someone who "knows."[12] Vital used the English phrases "he knows" and "he's got a strong mind" in speaking of the *ink'on*-endowed. (See his accounts in part 2.)

Both the person endowed with *ink'on* and the prophet are infused with their special kinds of knowing through their experiences with other-than-human beings. Yet from the understandings expressed by Dogribs in the 1960s, valid *ink'on* and valid prophecy are not the same. To infer from the evidential statements and behaviors of Dogribs that *ink'on* and prophecy differ in legitimating source, in effectual mode, and in goal is not to say that Dogribs, either as a culture-sharing collectivity or as individual thinkers, enunciate abstract distinctions between *ink'on* and prophecy. But for the inquirer into the structure of human affairs (or any other block of phenomena) elucidation begins in the teasing out of equivalencies and oppositions, of connections and disjunctions within the evidential mass. (The summation of the qualities of *ink'on* in this section is derived from the evidence in the accounts of *ink'on* presented in part 2.)

From experiences with other-than-human beings of the non-Christian world—experiences that until years are gained usually must remain secret or at least veiled—*ink'on* adepts come to know something that *empowers* them to *compel* change in human beings or in circumstances that affect human beings. Although the *ink'on* adept may compel circumstance for the welfare of the individual (restoration of health) or the group (control of game animals), the potency of *ink'on* itself is not intrinsically either moral and good or maleficent. Bringing what he "knows" to bear on his own intent, the *ink'on*-endowed aims to succeed in the hunt, cure, win over an opponent in the hand game, call up the wind, trace missing travelers, combat another's *ink'on*, inflict misfortune on or kill another with *ink'on*. With one exception, the *ink'on*-endowed imposes his effects on events and conditions apart from the exercise of volition on the part of other human beings. That exception is the curing of sickness that results from breach of moral norms. In order for health to be restored, the afflicted person or another person knowledgeable of the "wrong" behavior must choose to reveal the act that the curer-adept has divined. Here the demand of the *ink'on*-curer—that the sufferer examine his own moral state—parallels the demand of the prophet.

The prophets' experiences with the supramundane Christian world and

Fort Rae about 1910, looking east from Hudson's Bay Island to Priests' Island. The white two-story building is the mission. The buildings to the far left are across the "sny," on the mainland on Murphy's Point. Oblate Archives, Fort Smith.

its beings, to be publicly proclaimed when the prophets are deemed ready, *authorizes* them to *impel* change in others' *volition*, to bring others to *choose* to alter their thoughts and actions. The divinely authoritative message of the prophet intrinsically carries a moral charge, not only for the auditor who changes his or her behavior but especially for the moral health of the society.[13] Herein lies the ultimate distinction between the endowments and purposes of prophecy and those of power.

Afterword

The ethnography of the Dogrib prophet movement makes rather tame telling. None of the three prophets held out to the Dogrib people a millenarian dream. The prophets' ascents to the supernal Christian realm pale in contrast to the awesome death and return to life of Native American prophets of the last century. To the outsider, the prophets' messages would perhaps be more intellectually intriguing if they were syncretic of Christian and autochthonous beliefs. In the prophets' theologies the world of *ink'on* and the Christian cosmos do not merge. Their preachments and admonishments were incontrovertibly in line with those the Catholic fathers might enunciate from the pulpit. True, Jack's message carried an anti-white, nativistic thrust that those of Naidzo and

Chi lacked. And Jack's promotion of the ritual of the Alberta prophet dance brought the drama of group participation, while Naidzo offered only the theatrics of his style of storytelling and preaching and Chi simply the word pictures of his visions. Jack's mix of nativism, rite, and authoritarian leadership hinted at an ideological movement or a societal schism, but neither materialized.

As the fieldworker learns, no matter how small, "isolated," and "simple" a society, very diverse personalities are in action (Helm, DeVos, and Carterette 1963). In his own words each Dogrib prophet encapsulated distinctive aspects of his personality and character. Chi: "I was too shy to show myself. That's why I hid my dream from others." Jack: "If you don't believe me, you're going to go to hell." Naidzo, of becoming blind and crippled: "Do what you like. It'll do me good." From disparate psychological and emotional stances each came on his own path to prophecy, moved by a moral mandate bestowed through deeply personal revelatory experience.

PART TWO

Ink'on

When we were little kids we'd go to where an old man or an old lady stays. We'd ask for old stories. "Yes, but you've got to pay—cut wood, haul water." So we'd do all that, we'd bring enough for 'til morning. Then we'd go in the tipi and he would tell us all kinds of stories 'til our parents call us to bed.

Vital Thomas

4

One Man's *Ink'on*

The major impetus behind this collection of accounts of *ink'on* was not
the research program of the ethnographer but the pleasure of the native
consultant. Soon after meeting Vital Thomas in 1962 during my first
sojourn in Rae I realized that he had the interest and the temperament to
take on the role of key informant. Broadly, my field research emphases
were Dogrib society and polity present and past. But I also pursued with
Vital any questions raised by events, observations, conversations, and any
other happenings, as well as any topic Vital chose to bring up. We worked
together one to two hours every day. Since I paid Vital by the hour it was
in his financial interest to have the sessions run at least two hours. The
arrangement probably provided some motivation to introduce topics if
my agenda inquiries sagged. But his introductions of stories of *ink'on* into
our sessions flowed truly from his enjoyment of the stories and the sense
of wonder that they evoked in him.

In his younger years Vital had been the factotum and interpreter for the
Royal Canadian Mounted Police. (A brief life history concludes part 2.)
He was well versed in whiteman scheduling and work habits. His slow
deliberate speech usually allowed me to keep pace with his narration as
I wrote down his words, although often in a condensed form. I then typed
the transcription, usually the same day—a practice that might bring some
adjustment of the record for myself in the interests of clarity. The
accounts of *ink'on* that follow, then, are not reproductions of Vital's
narrations, but they are reasonable facsimiles for purposes of content. The
shifts in tense follow those in my transcriptions (which may have been
less grammatical than Vital's speech). Also, the notation [Q] derives from
the notation in my transcriptions that I asked a question at that point.

Over the years Vital and I worked together, two bush Indians of
roughly Vital's age made the effort to tell me that Vital didn't know
anything (or words to that effect). Since one of them was an absolute
monolingual, he had to commandeer a bilingual bystander to register his

Vital Thomas at age 58. Rae, 1962.

complaint. I understood their point of view. How could a man who had
spent his adult life living in Rae have all the experiences and know all the
things real bush Indians know? What *they* could not know was how
valuable was a collaborator like Vital—fully bilingual, a person who was
available every day at the time agreed on, interested, patient, and willing

to go over any point that needed clarification. Once, when a visiting Mountain Indian complained to Vital as interpreter that he didn't want to talk about kinship terms and practices, Vital barked back in Dogrib (free translation): "If you think this is boring, try being a linguistic informant!"

Luck and *magic* were words that some Dogribs fell back on when trying to refer to *ink'on* in English. Like other bilingual Dogribs, Vital was familiar with the expressions *medicine man* and *medicine,* and we at first used those phrases to introduce into our conversations the topic of *ink'on.* It is impossible to assign a succinct definition in English to *ink'on* except to fall back on the term *power,* so familiar to Americanists. Even after all these years, Franz Boas's characterization of "the fundamental concept bearing on the religious life of the individual"in aboriginal North America can hardly be improved on: "the belief in the existence of magic power, which may influence the life of man, and which in turn may be influenced by human activity. In this sense magic power must be understood as the wonderful qualities which are believed to exist in objects, animals, men, spirits, or deities, and which are superior to the natural qualities of man" (1910:366).

In Vital's usage, the signification of *ink'on* is protean. According to context, the word *ink'on* denotes a human being who is powerful, an other-than-human being that is powerful, and a powerfulness itself. The last sense appears to be the encompassing conception. But *ink'on* is not free-floating. It is lodged in, comes from, is exercised by some being (or possibly a natural phenomenon). In this sense, in order to delimit it as an instance or an attribute, it is better in English to think of *ink'on* as '*a* power' or '*a* powerfulness' rather than as 'power' unqualified by an article. The idea of the "spirit protector" or "spirit 'master' of the particular type of animal" (as in, for example, Müller 1989:102) as a major feature of the religions of the subarctic tribes set Nancy Lurie and me on the wrong verbal trail in our first few discussions with Vital about ideas around *ink'on.* In that idiom we phrased a couple of questions that were not meaningful to Vital, although he struggled to provide an answer. To use the term *spirit* in reference to an attribute of an animal or its species or in fact any kind of nonhuman entity did not register. Whether an animal comes to a human being in its own form or in human guise, it is the actual animal-being that is there and is speaking; no incorporeal essence or metaphysical entity, generic or individualized, is involved. That they are one-to-one interactions and relationships between human beings and real animal-beings came out when Vital strove to answer the question, "Can a man have more than one *ink'on?*" Yes, he replied,

"There are thousands and thousands of animals, foxes, wolves, dogs, bears . . ." There is no shortage of animal-individuals who may chose to be *ink'on* to some one human individual. Yet in some of the accounts the animal imposes strictures on the treatment of its entire kind.

From time to time I introduced confusion into our discussions by lapsing into speaking of "spirits" but the record of Vital's discourse shows that he would use the English word only when thinking of a human being's *inin*. Petitot translated the Chipewyan *inin* as *"esprit humain"* (1876:169). Morice wrote of a Babine Dene (who became a prophet) who "began to declare that he saw, floating in the air, over the heads of every one, a bodiless head with wings listening to the workings of each individual mind *(ni)"* (1971:239). (Oddly, as an Oblate priest who knew well the "Catholic ladder," Morice did not advert to the angels there depicted as bodiless heads with wings.) Vital spoke of "what [a human being] has in his mind, his spirit." It is the thinking, knowing, intentioning quality of being human, the human wit and will, that seems to be *inin* 'spirit'. In the stories of Akaitcho and Edzo, below, Vital phrased the capture of "Akaitcho's spirit" as *inin sicia* 'we will take his spirit'. A ghost is *ts'in.* Neither *inin* nor *ts'in* refers to 'soul'. Vital explained, "We didn't really have a name for soul before [the missionaries came]. For 'soul', we say *don dazin* 'our [i.e., human] breath'."

The accounts of *ink'on* from six other Dogribs that are presented along with Vital's are conceptually fully congruent with his. Those persons initiated their stories and information about *ink'on.* They wished to share their knowledge and I wish to acknowledge their contributions; thus I do not disguise their names.

The tenor of Vital's stories about getting *ink'on* and using *ink'on* as well as about being a person with *ink'on* should warn the reader off characterizing the other-than-human beings involved as guardian spirits or categorizing the human beings as shamans. The connotations that have accrued in the literature to those terms deflect understanding of Vital's presentation.

I speak of this collection of Vital Thomas' stories as one man's *ink'on.* But the reference is to his beliefs and cultural knowledge about *ink'on,* not his personal experience of it. I would never have asked Vital if he had experienced *ink'on.* But I was sure that he had not. I believe he would have stated or intimated it if he had. Vital missed that crucial time of life in the bush—he was seven years in the mission "orphanage" at Fort Resolution—when the maturing child may hope to meet in the bush the "stranger" or the animals who call to him, "Hey, hey, come . . ."

NOTE: *Several of Vital's stories involve Indians of the Great Bear Lake area. In most cases the context and the characters make it clear that the reference is to the regional band of Dogribs, Naidzo's band, who about 1914 switched their point of trade from Fort Rae to Fort Norman and Franklin. This Dogrib band is typographically identified as Bear Lake Indians, in contrast to the Bearlake Indians, a now distinct population "made up of the descendants of mainly Dogrib, Hare, and Slavey Indian groups who came into frequent contact with one another after the establishment of fur-trading posts at or near Great Bear Lake" (Gillespie 1981:310).*

5

Aspects of *Ink'on*

Getting and Becoming *Ink'on*

I ask Vital how a medicine man gets his power.

Well, his dream. Some of them, they dream. But some of them, when they are young they just happen to see something. Like a boy might go behind the point over there and here is a big bunch of people sitting and they say, "Hey, hey, come eat with us." And this young kid thinks it is true and he eats with them. And after, he plays with them. And when he is played out, he goes to bed. And when he wakes up, there is not a soul. Maybe just a bunch of ptarmigan there, or wolves. The wolves or the ptarmigan had made like persons.

And that is what makes a medicine man start. He says, "I been eating with wolves and now I can eat all kinds of food and never fill up myself."

Medicine men tell about their medicine and one says: "When I was a kid, I was walking and somebody called me, a stranger. 'Come on, little boy. We will show you how to make medicine'." Maybe there is a sick woman and the stranger sucks the sickness out and says, "When you grow up, you'll do same thing." And he tells the boy how to work medicine. Tells him everything. And when the boy gets old enough he does what the stranger tells him and starts to cure.

Like the Bear Lake Indians in the old days, if two, three guys visit them, they will feed them till they die, boil one whole moose, tell them to eat. They want to find out if the visitor is a good medicine man.

Like two men visit Bear Lake and shoot a moose before they get there. "Let's try to eat the moose so we won't have to pack anything tomorrow. If we clean up this moose tonight, we could do the same with what they cook for us [tomorrow]." And these fellows eat the entire moose in one night and one fellow says, "When I was a kid I used to eat and I would never get full because there was a bunch of wolves with me."

And when they got to the Bear Lake Indians and ate, they almost cleaned out the whole camp. If they were not medicine men, they were going to kill themselves with overeating. Bear Lake Indians in the olden times did that [stuff a visitor with food] all the time to see if he was a medicine man.

Between here and Great Bear Lake there were lots of caribou and the Indians from Bear Lake and from here came together and the Mountain Indians [Dene who exploited the eastern slopes of the Mackenzie Mountains and traded into Fort Norman] came too. They all met in a big camp. It was the time of year when the days are getting long. One fellow chased caribou with dogs. And the dogs raced down a hill and the man fell and broke his lower leg. And his dogs took him home. He was suffering pretty hard. They ask a Mountain man if he can do something. "For now, I couldn't do nothing unless someone kills a young moose." So next day the good hunters got a young moose. "We got it!" So the medicine man says, "Take this part of the bone [Vital indicates from knee to ankle] and cut it at the joint and clean it as good as you can. Don't leave any flesh on it."

So they do that. And he started to sing, sing, and pat the man's leg. And he put that bone right on top of the broken leg and starts to clap his hands. And the moose bone disappeared. And medicine man finished singing and he tell that man, "Stand up, start to walk." And the man started to walk. He placed that bone in the other one. Hard to believe that, but it's been done in front of lots of people.

Before the white man, without *ink'on* no Indians could be alive. They would have all starved to death and freeze. They got *ink'on* for hunting—caribou, moose. So lucky, they could get any kind of animal. But those guys, the hunting *ink'on,* couldn't cure nothing, unless themselves, anyway.

[Q] No, you can't see medicine. Maybe they carry feathers in the olden days.

[Q] Got to be young, five, six years old when you meet medicine. [On another occasion Vital said fifteen or sixteen years old.] You're not supposed to make medicine before you get married. If you start too young you won't live long. So he [the medicine being] tells you when to start it. Maybe there are two kids together someplace. One can see a bear, a man, and goes to him. The other kid won't be able to see it.

Before the white man, one time a little boy was hunting and he finds a bear hole. He sees a bear. The bear says "Gee, I like you. Come into my house overnight." So the boy goes into the bear's hole with the bear. The

"Got to be young, five, six years old when you meet medicine." Moïse Nitsiza. Lac la Martre, 1959.

bear says, "We'll have a sleep and go out tomorrow."

So the boy goes to bed with the bear, like one night. The bear says, "Don't go before I wake up." So they go to bed, and the kid is in the hole all winter. He never woke up. Finally the bear wakes him up. There is no snow—there is still ice, but no snow. Boy: "There was snow outside when I came in." Bear: "It's spring, you can go home now. You stayed overnight." And the boy thought it was just one night.

[Q] *Ink'on* is the word for medicine, medicine man, [human] spirit—all are the same word.

On another day I raised the question of women and ink'on. Oh, yes, women can have *ink'on.* They say that a woman's *ink'on* is stronger than a man's. [Q] Yes, some women cure with it, mostly [they do] doctoring. [Q] A woman gets *ink'on* same way as a man does. When a young girl has her first monthlies, got to build a little spruce tipi—say, as far from camp as from here to Philip Beaulieu's house. Out of the camp. Nobody should see her. Her mother builds a spruce tipi. The girl lives by herself till she gets older. And if she's lucky she going to get *ink'on.* That's the time. And when a girl's monthlies come, a young man should never get close to her. That's forbidden. If you get near you will be unlucky all your life.

In the olden days Bingo [a fourteen-year old in Vital's household] would have *ink'on* by now. But he wouldn't tell no one. *Ink'on* will tell him when to tell that he has *ink'on.* Maybe it is when he is grown up and is married and has two sons, or one son. Maybe then he can speak. *Ink'on* tells him that. But if you don't care about what *ink'on* tells you and mention it before you should, you won't live long.

If you get scared of your *ink'on,* you can't be a medicine man.

The Animals

In Vital's accounts, ink'on *involvements between people and animals are usually implied or imbedded rather than spelled out. Most, then, are to be found under other headings. Here are a few stories that treat specifically of animals.*

How the People Got Song and Dance from the Animals

In the course of chatting about tea dance songs, Vital said:
Some of the songs come from way back. Lots of them are animal songs. About a thousand years ago the animals were talking like us, that's the time they make those songs.

One time they had a dance. It was spring, the leaves just coming out. And each kind of animal had its own song. And they were singing, singing, were dancing, dancing. Two little boys were listening. And when they wake up, they thought it was just a short time. The boys didn't notice that the summer had passed. But there were no leaves on the trees by the time the animals finish dancing. The boys were listening and they said,

Tea dance: Dogribs and Slaveys at Fort Providence. The long shadows of dancers extending across the circle mark a new day after a summer's night of dancing. Fort Providence, 1967.

"We'll go when the animals finish dancing." And the animals were dancing, dancing and the boys were listening, listening, listening. And when the animals finished there were no leaves, it was late in September. So some of those songs come from the animals.

That story was told in 1962. In 1973 Vital recounted a similar tale:

Long ago, there was no kind of a dance, they say. And in the spring, early in May, there was a big group of Indians gathered. They don't know nothing about fur, they just follow the food. It was a great camp and all the young boys go out for ducks, prairie chickens—when [the chickens are] making dance. The boys all go and stay away overnight. But three young boys are missing. Finally, the people give up looking for them, they figure the boys are drowned, dead. So they move camp late in the fall, in September, to get close to caribou. They all follow one another, not like now. Nowadays, we got a different camp for hunting fur, but then no fur, just for food.

The leaves fall, there's frost on the ground. And the three boys come back. "Where you been?" "Oh, we just came to a dance so we started to dance." "Long time to dance!" "Oh, we just dance for three days." They think three months is three days! They brought back lots of songs. The headman tells them to sing. So the three dance the different songs, on and on. Only when the lake starts to freeze did they quit.

In 1976 Vital again told the tale of the prairie chickens, attributing it to one of his "grandfathers," Casimir. In this version, "Casimir used to tell the story that the people used to have no songs. In those days, the parents chased the boys into the bush overnight so they would get medicine or something. And when they were in the bush, they would hear the prairie chickens dance and hearing it they would go to see the good show of a dozen or so prairie chickens dancing. They'd sleep all day, and then hear the prairie chickens . . . "

The field notes continue: Vital goes on to describe the beauty of the prairie chicken dance. He shows how they spread their wings, put their heads down to dance, and how they drum so fast on the ground that "the rock shakes." He goes on to say that one of the birds is in a tree. And if it makes a noise all of them stop dancing (he indicates how they stop with their heads down, wings outspread, motionless), then the watcher in the tree makes another noise and they all start to dance again. When Vital and others were kids they used to lie very quietly and watch this.

Spider Ink'on

A man that dreams of spider *ink'on* is the strongest man for medicine because he could travel on the air and he could set nets anywhere. The spider talks to you and tells you how to make a living and if bad people are going to try to make you bad luck. Spider will tell you everything, what you should and shouldn't do.

Raven Ink'on

In recounting a curing by ink'on *that she saw as a girl, Elizabeth Mackenzie recalled that the curer held glowing coals in his mouth without being burned. Only those who have raven* ink'on *can do that.*

Lego and Loche

The loche (burbot, Lota lota) is the only purely freshwater cod. It has a whiskerlike barbel on the tip of the chin, the "thread" in Vital's story. The dramatic characterization of the loche by a nineteenth-century authority, quoted in McPhail and Lindsey, perhaps goes Lego's account one better: "It commonly lives under stones and in holes, waiting for its prey, and has come, from a rabbit-like habit, to be sometimes named the Coney-fish. Its instincts, however, are those of robber and pirate. It

Baby with loche. Rae, 1969.

waylays the female and the young brood . . . and is a terror to all small fishes"(1970:299).

Jeremy LaCorne's father was called Lego, a trader give him that name. That man was talking mostly about loche. Early in the spring the loche has been so long in the deepest part of the lake. In spring, he goes back to the shore. And when he see little fish [Vital gestures: two or three inches long] he follows the edge of the rock along the shore and where he finds a little corner, like [Vital indicates a wedge-shaped indentation], he goes in by his tail. His nose is out like a rock.

The loche has a thread on his chin. [Vital indicates a waving thread hanging down from the chin in the midline.] And he opens his mouth wide as he can and he starts to play with [move, wiggle] the little thread. He just move it and the young fish start to play with that, they think it is another little fish. When the little fish get so thick the loche gives a good swallow. And then he starts again and keeps on doing that. Then when he is filled up he goes away out in the deepest part of the lake and lays there for so many days. And when he gets hungry he comes back to the shore and does the same thing and little one-inch, two-inch fish follow the shore and come to his corner again.

And in the fall, before freeze-up, he goes out and caches it [the store of fishes in his gullet] out in a deep place and then he starts to travel and

"Boss for the Nets," Tamin K'awo, working on wood (as evidenced by the shavings). The birchbark hunting canoes, decked fore and aft, were the typical Dogrib craft of the era. Fort Rae, 1913. Photo by J. A. Mason, National Museum of Canada.

that's the time you get some loche once in a while. [And in winter] he lays down where his cache is. Just like he knows the calendar, in March he starts to travel again.

[Q] I don't know how Lego learned it but the old timers claim he is right. Maybe when he was a kid he traveled with the fish or something. Old LaCorne's father, that would be like Jeremy's grandfather, one time no one had nothing to eat. Everyone's got to set rabbit snares and him, he set some rabbit snares and came back with a loche [laughter]. Pretty hard to believe! Maybe Lego learned from his old father [laughter]. He got some rabbits, four or five, and one loche.

That's why Lego always talk about fish, because his dad know all about loche—caught one in a rabbit snare!

Boss for the Nets

"Blow-ups" of photographs made in 1913 by J. A. Mason (1946) posted on the walls of the Rae community hall in 1971 led to Mrs. Elizabeth Mackenzie's account about an old man featured in some of the photos. (See Helm 1981b on Mason's photos.)

His name was Tamin K'awo. His name [which Elizabeth thinks was not his "real" name but the one he was known by here] means "Boss for

Preparing a gill net. Rae, 1962.

the Nets." They called him that because he knows about fish. In those days people know by dreaming medicine. One winter there was no fish. And he made a medicine song and we see in his hand [Elizabeth cups her palm and makes circular motions over it] lots of little fish swimming round and round. [Q] Yes, after that people got fish in their nets. He was not from Rae. He came from Providence. [Mason identified him as "Tinite, a Slavey shaman."]

One time Vital commented: They say that there is a lake between here on earth and heaven. And there is a point of land that sticks out into the lake and if you follow it you will be a great medicine man. And if you see a fish net there you will always be lucky for catching fish. This place is called Yak'eti, Heaven Lake.

Proscriptions Imposed by Animals

I ask Vital about not eating the meat of an animal that has talked to you.

You can eat and you can kill the animal unless he tells you, "You're not supposed to kill me." If the animal didn't mention that, then you can eat him. You can do just like us [like everyone else does].

Mostly bear—you're not supposed to kill or eat its meat unless you're very hard up. Like caribou, somebody dreams about caribou. The caribou says, "If you want to be lucky for caribou, you are not supposed to eat my head." So lots of guys, even 'til now, don't eat caribou head. [A more extended discussion is presented in the next section.]

In the course of a wide-ranging conversation Elizabeth Mackenzie brought up several topics that apparently she thought might interest me, including the following:

Some people are scared of bear. They don't eat it. You could not even say the word *bear* in front of Alexis Arrowmaker's grandfather. Nobody used that word in front of him, he don't like it.

People learn of these things in dreams. Beaver, too. Even me. When I was a girl I was just like a white person. I did not know about these things. But one time a beaver came in a dream and said, "I don't like for a young lady to wear me around her slippers." [Elizabeth is referring to the beaver-fur cuff on moccasin slippers.] Since that time I have never worn beaver fur.

This led to an anecdote stemming from a trip in 1950 by Elizabeth, her daughter, and evidently a number of other persons to Fort Resolution for tuberculosis X-rays. One of the girls from Rae was wearing mukluks trimmed with beaver fur. One of the Resolution women told Elizabeth, "We are all scared to wear beaver." According to Elizabeth, none of the Resolution women wear beaver.

Hunters' *Ink'on*

Wedzitxa

In the olden days you got to have *wedzitxa.* He was something like *wek'axots'edeh,* like old Murphy was before Treaty [see Vital's auto-biography, chap. 8]. After the white men came, we had *wek'axots'edeh* right up to treaty. You could call him *denekawi.*

Wedzitxa is a old, old, old name before the white men came. [Q] He was something like *yambati* but he did different work. *Yambati* was for fighting. *Wedzitxa* was for hunting, we got to have one person we follow. *Yambati* was only for war [see "Yambati," in chap. 7]. *Wedzi* is 'caribou', *txa* is 'shooter'. A real *wedzitxa* could go in the night and make three marks on a caribou's foot and not wake it up. Some could make one or two marks but only a real one could make three. He has power to do that. He'd tell his boys in the morning, "I went over last night and you'll see a female caribou with three marks on its foot. That's me!" Sure enough, next day they all watch at the butchering and they find one female with three marks on the foot.

[Q] Yes, *wedzitxa* hunted alone. He goes alone, others might scare the caribou away. He's the only one can handle them. It don't matter how cold it is, caribou aren't scared of him. [This is a reference to the difficulty of approaching caribou or moose because sound carries so far in very cold weather.] He knows power. The other men watch him kill caribou from way on top of a hill.

There were [only] a few *wedzitxa*. The real *wedzitxa*, he goes to the caribou and while they are laying down. The real *wedzitxa* could make three marks on the foot of a caribou without waking up the caribou. That means that his *ink'on* comes from the caribou. That's why he's so lucky. Not many can make a mark on a caribou's foot.

Wek'axots'edeh, that's like a leader.

Wedzitxa, this man feeds the whole crowd. If we got one *wedzitxa* we don't have to worry much, it's just like he owns a farm. Like if he see caribou, he just kill every one, fifty, a hundred.

[Q] A real life *wek'axots'edeh* would be like Murphy before treaty, everybody follows his order. If you ask an old-timer, "Wonder which way we should go?" The old-timer would say, "We can't say much until we hear from *wek'axots'edeh*, we got to wait for his orders."

In May 1971 Beryl Gillespie visited Naidzo the Bear Lake Prophet at Fort Franklin and recorded some of his stories and reminiscences. Two months later Vital translated from the tape Naidzo's account of wedzitxa. *Unlike Vital (who was questioned on the point), Naidzo made no distinction between* wedzitxa *and* wek'axots'edeh.

Before the white man came, we had nothing to fish with and no gun, no ice chisel, no line. Then, we follow *wedzitxa*. That's what I'm going to talk about.

We used moose or caribou horn for chopping wood and ice. *Ink'on*, that's all we had. That's how we hunt for a living, we depend on *ink'on* for hunting caribou, moose. And the luckiest man, he feeds everybody.

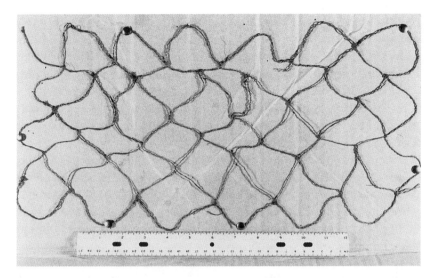

Segment of gill net made of willow bast (inner bark), made by Philip Huskey's mother-in-law. Dessication and the years have loosened the twist of the cordage. Since a net of willow bast could never be allowed to dry out, summer or winter, few families could manage to keep one. By Naidzo's account, before the Indians got manufactured netting twine the family that had a bast net accrued followers. Rae, 1962. Collected by June Helm.

Wedzitxa is like the master for caribou and moose. He is so great, so powerful. Where he sees caribou, he dresses himself like a caribou and walks among caribou and just chases the bull away and leaves the females. He shoots the females with bow and arrow. When he gets all the females, the bull is waiting for the females so he is easy to kill. So he kills every caribou in the bunch. So that is how he has the name Follow Man, *wek'axots'edeh* 'we follow him'. That's the way God help us, with *ink'on*, because we didn't know anything else. When we're hard up, the man that gets luck dreaming about caribou or moose, that's how we save one another.

Before *mola* [the white man] comes, that's the only way we live. Hard, but that's the way we did it. But after *mola*, its different—he has all the equipment for trapping, hunting, fishing. After *mola*, no more *wek'axots'edeh* and no more *wedzitxa* because we have all the white man's stuff. We had a hard time in the old days, before the white man. If anyone gets meat—moose, bear—we feed one another. We got no equipment like now. Still, God help us. That's why we were so happy, them days. We feed one another so good. It's different now.

In the summer of 1979 Vital translated for me a tape he had made of Bruno Gaudet a year and a half before. At that time Bruno Gaudet (baptized 1887) was perhaps the oldest man in Rae. Here is Bruno's account of wedzitxa.

In the olden days, before the white man, we follow the caribou. Everyone move to where they could find caribou. And everyone gather together to find caribou. That way they were making a living.

In the olden days, it was pretty hard—snow, really cold, you couldn't get close to caribou. No guns, only bows and arrows. But there was *wedzitxa*. We tell him, "There are lots of caribou but we can't get close." *Wedzitxa* says, "You stay here, I'll walk over." The caribou were not scared of him because he was a great medicine man. He cleans all the caribou he sees. And when he kills all the caribou he divides it among whole crowd, the same amount to all. And all knew he was a great hunter—that's why they respect him. And that's the way we go through the winter.

After the white man comes with guns, Indians bought muzzle loaders and they done the same thing. If they see a bunch of caribou they all follow and wait for the caribou. They tell *wedzitxa* the same thing. If caribou are on a lake, *wedzitxa* says, "Let me play with them first." And he does and Indians all follow with guns and kill all the caribou on the lake. That's the way he was, the old *wedzitxa*.

Etano and the Caribou

"Old Fort" was the original Fort Rae, founded in 1852. Its site is about fifteen air miles from the present Fort Rae, down the North Arm of Great Slave Lake. (This is not Old Fort Island featured in another story.) Russell visited it in 1893–94 and met Etano, whom he characterized as "an old Indian named Tenony, formerly the engaged hunter for [the Hudson's Bay Company post at] Rae, now generally called 'The Fort Hunter'" (1898:80). Russell noted in 1893–94 that the caribou "are not abundant in winter around Rae, where they were killed by hundreds ten years ago" (p. 226). During a canoe trip to Old Fort in 1970 Vital told about the death of Etano, who was Vital's mother's father.

Etano died at Wetcho River between the barrens and Russell Lake. Dying, he said they could bury him there. But if they wanted the caribou to come to the fort [what is now Old Fort] as they used to, they should take the headskin of the youngest caribou and place it in his coffin, then take him back for burial at the fort. "That means [said the dying man] that there will be lots of caribou next year. I feel sorry because the caribou don't come often around the fort. Next year, if you see caribou, you'll believe me." So they did as he said. It was a long trip, over a hundred

Harry Bearlake, Naidzo's brother-in-law, applying melted spruce gum to the sinew lashing holding the feathers on an arrow. Vital is helping. Rae, 1970.

miles. And they buried him in the graveyard at the fort. And the next fall, in October or November, the caribou were so thick among the houses and all through the graveyard! That must be strong medicine!

Forty years later I told Dodo Lafferty about it. Dodo was living at Old Fort. And Dodo says, "I'm going to try another attempt at] luck with the old man. I'll save a young caribou headskin and put it on his grave." So he did, he put a caribou headskin on the grave and talked to the grave, to the old man: "Your poor grandchildren are all starving, they need meat. Can you help us just once more?" That fall the caribou were so thick around Russell Lake and Old Fort point! Thousands! And that was the last time.

And the time in 1947 when we put the cross at Old Fort for the hundred years, there were still some old timers alive, like Pierre Liske. And the Father brought them all to Old Fort—forty or forty-five kickers [outboard motors]. We cleaned the graveyard. And Pierre Liske says, "I'd like to see Grandfather"—that's Etano—but we couldn't find nothing. It [the grave site] was too old, it had dropped down or something. Pierre wanted to ask for some more help, but we couldn't find it.

[Q] Yes, Pierre Liske was relations to Etano. Pierre and I called one another *kinde* [older brother] and *seci* [younger brother], cousins.

Vital must have been mistaken on the 1947 centenary. Neither the year of the founding of the fort by the Hudson's Bay Company nor that of the mission matches.

Hunters' Ink'on *and Proscriptions on Women's Food*

I ask if there are foods generically forbidden to all women or to all men. There are not, but Vital tells of how an individual's ink'on *may proscribe a certain food from that hunter's kill.*

Suppose there is a good hunter who is lucky for caribou, because he's got *ink'on* against caribou. And his *ink'on* tells him that a woman shouldn't eat caribou head or maybe caribou heart or whatever. Any other kind of meat [of the caribou], but not the head or the heart. [Q] His wife is going to tell this to the other women of the camp [i.e., the proscription extends beyond the women of the hunter's own family]. When the women boil caribou head for the men they ask if women can eat it before they serve it. Some men might say it's okay, another might say no. [Q] It is just the caribou killed by the hunter whose *ink'on* has told him women should not eat the head. If another man in the same camp kills a caribou, that caribou head can be eaten by the women.

There's one man here in town like that but I don't want to mention his name because he won't like it . . . he's been talking against me . . . [this is put rather vaguely but this seems to be why Vital is especially wary of telling who]. He's a man of thirty-eight or forty. Anytime he kills a caribou, no one, especially women, is going to touch the head, the heart, or the throat bones. [Q] It's okay for men [but not for women] to eat the head. But even the killer, *nobody,* eats the throat bones. That's one thing you shouldn't laugh about. So they [the people] don't like to mention it.

Some men, if *ink'on* doesn't tell them anything, women can eat all parts of anything they kill.

Vital has never heard of ink'on *proscribing a certain food for children in general but is led to discuss food restrictions and other precautions that children should observe.*

Suppose you raise a boy in the old time way. There's lots of things he shouldn't eat until he grows up. Like he shouldn't eat rabbit's ears, because if he does when he grows up his ears will make all kinds of noise [internally] and he'll be scared to hunt. He'll be nervous when he grows up [Vital indicates with his fingers how a rabbit's ears are always twitching]. [Q] Oh, yes, there's lots more. The leg bone of the caribou [Vital indicates his own thigh], a boy growing up is not supposed to eat it, especially the marrow. Because when chasing caribou you'll have a weak leg, you can't keep up with the caribou or moose or whatever. And when you're young, you're not supposed to drink too much water—that's a bad habit, you can't run because you'll sweat too much and be thirsty. Oh, lots of things, especially young boys growing up, they forbid lots of things. [Q] Yes, girls too, about the same. A girl not supposed to go near young brother's bedding. She got to work just inside the door, not where brother's bedroll is or he'll be unlucky. And they don't want a girl to [walk a]cross caribou blood or whatever—any kind of game blood.

Family Food Proscriptions

I commented to Vital that I had been told that the Navajos, unlike their northern cousins, will not eat fish. Vital quite promptly decided on the reason for this:

It is probably because they all come from one family. Some families here maybe won't eat bear. Another family won't eat jackfish. [Q] *Ink'on* tells them. Some people will not eat bear meat right now because their parents didn't eat it. They throw it away or give it away. And some won't eat muskrat. They will kill it but they won't eat it. I think that's why the Navajo can't eat fish.

Curing with *Ink'on*

John Bighead Cures Vital

Vital identified a youthful man in a photo taken at Fort Resolution in 1913 as John (Jean) Bighead, Kwitco (Helm 1981b: fig.8). From other remarks by Vital, it seems that the incident recounted here probably occurred in the early 1920s.

I had pneumonia about a hundred miles from here. We were in the bush for caribou. I was in bed for three days, at last I couldn't talk. It was too far to Rae to take me to town. So they ask John Bighead if he can help me. He says, "I'll try to, but it is pretty hard to say—I haven't made medicine since I was a young man."

I was so sick I couldn't hardly breathe. I didn't eat for three days, lots of pain. They put a hot stone on my chest [Vital indicates a spot over the left lung, low]. The stone was so hot it burned through my shirt, but I was suffering so much I didn't even feel the heat.

The man [Bighead] starts to sing and says, "It is only my dogs that tell me the truth. I'm going to take the pain out of this man. If I take it all, my dogs will yowl. If I don't take it all, my dogs won't yowl."

And he moved his hands all up my body. [Vital indicates a patting, working motion of both hands, starting at about the hips and working all the way up the body.] And he moved his hands all up my body to the top of my head and [Vital claps hands above his own head to illustrate] then he shows his hand and says, "Here we are. This is what you asked me to take out." And he had something white in his hand [Vital indicates something about the size of half of his thumb] like foam. "But my dogs don't tell me yet. If I didn't get all the pain out of this man, they won't yowl." All at once the dogs yowl and he says, "Now I took it all!"

And the next day I didn't feel any pain, nothing. And that man said, "If the doctor keep you, he is going to keep you one month, two months. But me, just one night!" [Actually, at this time there was no doctor available to Dogribs.]

The big medicine men are all dead now. Medicine men are not very strong now, getting weak. A strong medicine man is *ink'ondeh*. When they try to cure somebody, got to have lots of people around—three, four men anyway, to prove he does it. [Q] You pay *ink'on* whatever he asks for—tobacco, shells, dog harness, sleigh. If he says he can't cure you, you don't pay him.

[On another occasion Vital said that the *ink'on* curer] cures by singing. But he's got to do it with pay [has to receive payment]. The right pay is moccasins with porcupine quills or a fish net. If you [the curer] don't get pay or you try to use the same words on your own without *ink'on* saying [that you can], you just hurt yourself. Bad luck. [Q] *Ink'on* comes when you start to sing. If you [the curer] are paid right, *ink'on* comes when called.

I once asked if ink'on *for the hand game (see below) was unique to the game. Vital explained:* The doctor *ink'on* knows all about gamblers. The doctor *ink'on* knows about everything except hunting.

Toby Bearlake Requires "The Truth" to Cure a Fornicator

At the end of this eyewitness account Jim Fish (b. 1912) revealed the sick man's identity, but in order to sort out the two referents of he *in the narrative I have assigned a pseudonym to the protagonist early in the story. A truncated version of the account follows. Jim Fish learned his English during a five-year stay in a tuberculosis ward in Edmonton, which accounts for his use of "standard English" for bodily functions.*

Sometimes if you do something wrong you get a disease. To get well, you got to tell the truth about what you've been doing. He [the *ink'on*-curer] tells you what you've been doing, how you got the disease. Sometimes you don't want to tell, but he goes over what you've been doing for about the last twenty years. If you still don't want to tell, he can't do nothing. There is a whole bunch of people in the tent, you know. Some women don't want to tell the truth in front of their husbands. And some of the guys don't want to tell in front of the people. In order to cure the sick person, you try to push him to tell the truth. A fellow [Joe] got sick. He couldn't have a bowel movement or pass water. So he asked Old Toby Bearlake to help him and he offered Toby one white fox [pelt] to pay him. The old man began to sing. And Toby told Joe, "You got that sickness from [because of] one of the girls." But Joe didn't want to tell.

I was with Joe [when he did "something wrong"]. We were starting to move camp. We were traveling [by dogsled] on a lake and it was getting dark. He had a girl with him and they went around a point. Joe had intercourse with the girl there and the old man knew it, that's what he was singing. The old man told Joe what he [Joe] had been doing. He said, "You went around the point there and you had one fellow with you." It was me! I told Joe to tell the truth. But Joe was kind of shy. I said to him, "You got to tell the truth, that you had intercourse with that girl." And then the girl came in. "Why don't you tell the truth?" the girl said. "You were with me behind the point and you know what you did but now you're shy to tell the truth. Why don't you tell the truth like I am doing?" And then Joe told the truth and that old man cured him right away. When daylight broke we took Joe out and he had a bowel movement.

Vital told of another kind of "wrong" behavior that in the "olden days" might bring sickness: thinking bad thoughts about or saying something "wrong" about a dead person. "The ghost will follow you and you get sick. So you find a medicine man and if you confess . . . you chase the ghost away with ink'on *and get cured. "*

The Ethnologist's Curing Story Boomerangs

When Vital Thomas and I began working together in 1962 I told him, as a pump-priming ploy, a story I had heard when among the Slavey of a mother-in-law who saved her son-in-law's life by confessing that he had forced her to have sexual intercourse. My account was hardly more extensive than the one in the prior sentence. Five years later Vital had obviously forgotten the source of the story. In fact, if he had not specified the Slavey setting I would not have recognized it as my own story, so richly was the tale fleshed out, including much more dialogue than here presented.

The story emerged as a case in point as Vital was explaining how the curing ink'on *works:*

Medicine men can catch things [find out about something] since two years back. It's funny, they can tell you right straight. [Question on how they know what makes someone sick.] Oh, something you might eat you shouldn't, or you might pass over a bear hide or bear blood. [Q] It is just knowing, finding out what causes the trouble, that can cure it.

There was old Slavey medicine man. A young fella married a widow's daughter and his wife was knocked up so he couldn't get no tail. He went after his mother-in-law. "I'm not well," she told him. "That don't make no difference," he tell her. "If I get some tail, I'll be alright." She says, "Well, I told you I'm not well," but he just help himself and got all he wanted. After a while he got sick and the medicine man came there and started to make medicine. "You done something you shouldn't do, that's why you're like this. If you confess I can cure you." But he [the sick man] didn't like to mention it in front of his wife. The medicine man says, "If you don't confess, you're gonna die." There was a whole bunch there. They do that when someone's sick, to see medicine man making medicine. "You gotta mention it," he says. Just then the old lady come in by herself. "Son-in-law, I told you I wasn't well and you said 'Never mind'. Tell the truth, you came after me." "At last!" the medicine man says. "Now we know! That's the way to cure you." You can't hide nothing from them fellas.

After a couple of more years Vital again gave this story. My notes on it were minimal. After another two or three years he told the tale again, dropping the Slavey attribution. To Vital's obvious puzzlement, I took almost no notes at all.

Cree Medicine

Cree Nahdi *and Dogrib* Ink'on

The Crees handle root, *nahdi*. They are different from Indians [Dogribs, Dene]. They use roots. We don't call that *ink'on*, we call it root—*nahdi*, like a serpent, something. [There are no snakes in Dogrib country.]

To make love, they put root in a cigarette, blow the smoke at a girl and if she breathes that smoke she's going to chase that guy. Run 'til she catches the boy. That's what mostly they used to do. Even 'til now they teach one another, these young boys. When I was young, a Cree try to sell me love medicine for ten dollars. He says, "You won't have no trouble to make love." I said, "I don't want to buy it. If my mother finds out she is going to kill me." Don't need medicine to get a girl, anyway.

Some Dogribs could do that, but just with spirit, power [i.e., no root or object involved]. Dogribs [just as a folk remedy] could boil "rat root" [part of an aquatic plant] and with the juice could cover all your body and the man who really knows how to use the root could cure you.

A couple of weeks later, Vital enlarged upon the Cree.

Boniface

I knew a great Cree medicine man when he was dying. A bunch went to Fort Resolution, forty-four dog teams from Snowdrift, Rocher River, all over, and bunch of five men came from Fort Smith. [These would all be Chipewyan Dene.] In those days the mail was carried with dog teams. We all meet and stay at the same house at Resolution. An old man was dying, TB I guess. He was known as a great medicine man. He was a half-breed Cree named Boniface. One evening five boys from Smith come to see the old fellow. He knows them and he says, "I like to see you guys. The way I feel, I'm gonna die. It's my heart. Can't cure my heart. When a man's heart is bad he can't cure that. But I'm not sorry, I've had my fun in this world. Would some of you young guys want to buy medicine?" They say, "That's what we come for." He says, "I got three different kinds, the highest is twenty-five dollars, the second is fifteen dollars worth, and the third is ten dollars worth. If you buy twenty-five dollars worth I'll tell you how to use it." One young fella says, "Uncle, I want to buy twenty-five dollars." The old man says, "Good, I won't be using it myself anymore and you won't be sorry you bought it." He takes a sackful of little roots and he says, "S'pose you hunt moose, you find the tracks and can't keep up with it. Just crumble a little piece on the track and the moose will turn back, come back to you, you don't have to hunt for him. Same way with fur too, just one little crumb will help you trap a thousand dollars worth. You won't be sorry. Same thing for girls. I wouldn't be using this medicine, but I know any young guy in this world is thinking of girls. You won't have to chase them, they chase you. S'pose you like a girl and she won't even look at you. You don't say nothing, just put a crumb in your pipe or cigarette and go out. You won't go far, the girl catches you in no time."

Two of those guys bought twenty-five dollars worth, one bought fifteen dollars worth, and the youngest, ten dollars worth. Gee whiz, they were glad. I was same age as them, about eighteen, and my bed was alongside the old man. Those fellows say, "Hullo, Vital, what's the matter with you? What's wrong with you, you don't buy any medicine even for girls?" I says, "My mother always tell me not to buy something that don't belong to me. I can get girls without roots. I don't think I need root to get girls, I'm a young fellow. If I want to kiss a girl I don't need root." The old fellows with me say, "You're right!" Everybody was pleased with me. And now I'm the only one alive, those five all died a long time ago.

Our parents, the old fellows used to teach us everything, just like the mission. It's all true, they know that hundreds of years before the priests come here. "Keep away from girls," they say, "if you want to be good hunter." So many years they are talking and acting that way but that's all gone now. Now you tell young fellows things like that they think you're kinda crazy, just laugh. My parents [i.e., relatives] say, "Some girls are unlucky and some are lucky, but you can never tell, so best to keep away."

6

"The Highest Men for *Ink'on*"

Through the years Vital Thomas' expositions on ink'on *ordinarily took the form of narrative stories about particular characters in which occasionally a generalizing remark was imbedded. Once he offered a broad summation:*

A real *ink'on* person knows all about the sky. They say there's a lake up there and he knows all the points of land and the water. He can tell you everything that you could think of. He knows about the roots underground and about what it is like under the water. He knows about the wind. He can sing and make wind blow. If you need help, maybe your kicker breaks and you got no way to get home, you say to one of those men, "Save our lives!" and he start to sing which way the wind should blow.

The attributes of ink'on—*triune* ink'on *as a power, a human person, and an animal or other-than-human being—emerge in Vital's tales about "the highest men for ink'on." These men are known as* ink'ondeh *('big* ink'on'), done ink'on elin, *or* ink'on elin. *Lurie (field notes) recorded the same usages as Vital's among the Lac la Martre Dogribs. (Scott Rushforth, p. c., reports that the Bearlake Dene also use the comparable phrase* dene 'įk'ǫ hęlį *'person is powerful'.) In the following tales we meet several of these* ink'ondeh *by name: One Foot in Heaven (alias One Foot in Hell), Slim Ekawi, Gaxieh, Alphonse W, Ts'ocia, Godeh, Got'ocia, Old Marrow, and Beaverhook.*

One Foot in Heaven, Alias One Foot in Hell

A medicine man is called *ink'on*. The highest man for medicine is *ink'ondeh*.

Suppose men have gone from Rae to Resolution and are supposed to be back but aren't back. If we can find an *ink'on*, we pay him some chewing tobacco or pipe tobacco or shells and ask him to find out where those guys are. Are they safe? When will they be back? And then the medicine man starts to sing. More men come, and the more men come around, the more he sings. All of them are watching him.

And he says: "I'm starting from here and here is a channel." And we say, "That's Frank's Channel!"

And he says, "And from there there is a bay and after that a point with a few little houses on it."

And the men ask, "Old Fort?"

"Yes, and from there, past that point, there is a small island . . ." And he keeps on going. "I'm going to take the left side of the lake first and them come up the other side." He tells the men where he is at each moment and he keeps going till he gets to Yellowknife Bay. From there he says, "I'm going to cross the bay [Vital continues geographical descriptions] and there are islands . . ." And he describes each place and we tell him what it is. And he gets close to Gros Cap and he yells "Hey! hey!" and starts to jump up, "Here we are!" And he has found the men.

In those days we are waiting for the York boat to arrive. The Bay [Hudson's Bay store] is often short of supplies, and when supplies come in the first men that get there get all the smokes, tea, and the rest of the men don't get anything. We are hungry for smokes, tea, and we ask the medicine man to see where the York boat is and when it is coming.

And he start to sing, sing. "Here we are, they are having a rest. Before daylight, they are going to pull out. They'll be coming, coming and they'll be here just before sundown."

And we tell him, "Don't tell us a lie or we will never pay you again."

"You'll see, the flag will go up before sundown!" In those days, it was a big time when the York boat came, all the men rowing. And the Bay would put the flag up on the pole when the boat came.

So we wait. Next day, we all stand on the top of the rock by the Bay and all watch toward Frank's Channel for the York boat. A dozen men rowing, gee whiz, it looks good! And the old man says, "Who's lying now?"

[Q] Yes, I saw this happen. [Q] The medicine man's name was One Foot in Heaven. His father gave him that name because he would be the top man for medicine. The whites changed his name to One Foot in Hell. He has two sons alive today.

[Q] A medicine man uses the drum at the beginning, when he starts to sing. [Q] All the story is in singing. The medicine man sings all through but uses the drum just at the beginning.

And when fall comes, they come to see One Foot in Heaven. "We'd like to hear caribou news. How far is caribou?" And they give him three or four shells, tobacco.

"A dozen men rowing, gee whiz, it looks good!" Dogribs in York boat, Great Slave Lake. Near Fort Resolution, 1913. Photo by J. A. Mason, National Museum of Canada.

And he starts to sing and does the same [as in the York boat search]. "We're here [at Rae] and now I'm going and here are narrows and here is a point on the left side." And we tell him which point it is. "And there is a big island and another point with a house" and that is in the middle of Russell Lake. And then he goes to LeJeunesse Bay and follows the road [route] and [much geographic detail]. And before he gets to edge of the woods, "Here is caribou!"

And we say, "To make sure, can you pinch hair from the caribou?" And he says "I'll show you!" and he starts to sing more. Medicine men got something they send out—"I'll wait till my medicine comes back," and he sings. And then he jumps, "My medicine is coming back!" And he leaps and [Vital demonstrates] claps his hands over his head and, "Here! Here is caribou hair!"

[Q] Yes, I saw this. [Q] One Foot in Heaven died about 1934. [Q: Are any medicine men alive today?] Bruno Wanazah [a son of One Foot in Heaven] is good. He could do the same thing for caribou now.

In 1967, five years after Vital recounted these stories about One Foot in Heaven, he was chatting with Lurie and me when Alphonse Eronchi (b. 1919) came in. We had started to discuss the ethnographers' difficulty in recognizing descent lines through the surname, as three or four brothers may each have a different surname. This led to my reference to one of the more intriguing names here, namely, One Foot in Hell. Alphonse began to talk animatedly:

One Foot in Hell was the biggest medicine man in Rae. When he cured he had to tell how he became a medicine man. And then he would take the bad spirit out of the sickness. The story that One Foot in Hell told about himself was: "At the beginning I came from heaven. I was in heaven and I was made into a feather. And then through a tube I was blown to earth. On earth I began to search for a mother. When I found her, I began to grow in her womb. When I got born, I didn't remember what went before. I had to learn the language. And the wolves and the animals were teaching me everything. I came from heaven like from the moon, so that is my name."

The priest did not like this story, so he changed One Foot in Heaven's name to One Foot in Hell.

One time One Foot in Hell cured old Madelaine D. That woman was very sick, not able to work. One Foot in Hell came. He said, "You got to tell me about your past. You must have been with a man. You've got to tell and I'll cure you. It is killing you." And Madelaine said, "My husband went to visit his snares in a canoe and while he was gone I was lying down and Louis [a métis] came in. He lay down beside me and rolled a cigarette for me and gave it to me to smoke."

When One Foot in Hell heard that he jumps up and down, up and down, and he says, "That's right! That's right! Louis tried to root you. I am going to take that root out of you."

In remarks accompanying the development of the One Foot in Hell story, Alphonse and Vital agreed that Cree medicine power practice characteristically involves the use of roots (and other objects?) but Dogribs rely only on unembodied ink'on. As Alphonse's brother Jim Fish said on another occasion, "We just use the head." As he spoke, with thumb and forefinger Jim turned an imaginary knob by his temple, as if turning up the incandescence of the mantle of a gas lamp.

Madelaine was lying there naked to the waist. One Foot in Hell took the drum and he laid it all over her breasts and chest. Then he sang and sang and he sucked through the drum and then he spit green stuff out in his hand. You couldn't look at it. It was dirty. "That's the poison. That's what's been killing you."

"At the north end of the world there is a big mouth, at the end of the world there is a big mouth with big teeth [Alphonse illustrated with his hands how the mouth and teeth open and close]. I have been there. I have seen that. I am going to swallow [just as the great mouth and teeth swallow]."

Three times One Foot in Hell done that. "Now there is no more poison inside you. You will be very sick tomorrow. But after that you will be okay. Just eat soup. Tomorrow I'll make juice from roots for you. Drink one cup a day for three days."

Alphonse: And at the end of the month I seen her walking around and chopping wood. [Q] I saw that about thirty years ago. [Perhaps forty years is closer.] I had just come out of the convent [apparently the mission school at Resolution] and I didn't believe that sort of thing. I thought it was superstition. But then I saw it happen.

One Foot in Hell used to tell us, "The fish, the birds, even the wood, talks to me. When I was young, I expected things like that to happen to me. I enjoyed it so when I was young. I make me into an eagle one time. I flew over the land looking everywhere and my wings made a big noise. [Alphonse gestures with his arms to indicate the soaring flight of the eagle]. One time when I was a kid, I walked around at night. And I heard crying, a kind of moaning. I couldn't see anyone. Finally it sounded like it was coming from a tree. It was the tree crying. 'Hello, stranger. I am dying. Can you help me?' The tree had a big lump growing on it. The tree was very sick. It was asking me for help. I said, 'You're not human, can you be sick too?' 'Sure', said the tree. I took my ax and slapped the lump. It disappeared. The tree said, 'Thank you'."

One Foot in Hell said, "Only one thing is dangerous for me, the food that a dog has eaten from. That is poison for me."

Alphonse now continues the narrative in his own person: It was fall and the people from Snare Lake met One Foot in Hell on the road [trail]. All of them gave meat to people. And William C gave meat to One Foot in Hell. William had the meat from a dog in his sleigh. He said, "Here, Grandfather." William had forgotten that a dog had eaten on that meat, and the old man didn't notice. He was very sick. When he got home, he couldn't help himself. He said, "I'm going to die. You can't help me." And he died.

Vital interjects: That's something that's poison for all [Dogrib] Indians. Even myself. Even if a dog just licks off a plate, you got to throw it away. It don't matter if you are a medicine man.

Alphonse: Even a brand new pail, you got to throw it away. There is a bad spirit in the dog. William C killed that old man. He's the one that did it. An Indian can't eat any part of an animal that has been touched by a wolf, same as with a dog.

Slim Ekawi and the Eskimos

Toby Bearlake's father was one of the head men *[ekawi]* for Bear Lake. *Ekawidare*—'Slim Ekawi'. Tall man. [In a later year, Vital decided 'tall' was perhaps a better translation]. And he was a great medicine man so everybody was scared of him. There is a story about him. They [some Dogribs] made a trip to an Eskimo camp. And in them days the Eskimos had never seen the police or mission. They were just like wild men in the bush.

The Copper Eskimos are the Inuit whom Dogribs occasionally encountered in the barrens. The Copper Eskimos "came into contact with civilized law for the first time in 1916 when a patrol of the Royal Northwest Mounted Police arrested and deported the murderers of . . . two French missionaries" (Jenness 1922:90).

And these Indians, when they came to Eskimo camp the other two men said, "Eskimos are dangerous. Let's don't go to that camp." But Bearlake says, "Might as well go. They can't do much. When I was young, I met everybody in the world and they couldn't kill me." That's what he got in his mind, his spirit.

The Eskimos gave them something to eat. Then the Eskimos start a quarrel with them. One Eskimo grabs a bow and arrow and he is going to shoot Ekawidare. Ekawidare says, "Go on, shoot!" The Eskimo tried and he couldn't spring his bow. So he throws the bow and arrow away and takes a muzzle-loader. And Ekawidare says, "Shoot!" and the Eskimo points the gun but he can't do nothing. He tried hard but the gun started to melt. So he had nothing to fight with, so he made friends.

So you know how strong the medicine Ekawidare got.

Gaxieh

A big medicine man can catch storms. He sits on the storm, puts it under him and sits on it. A real medicine man can save other fellows' lives. Old Marrow's uncle, old Gaxieh, the son of Edzagwo, could do that.

They [some Dogribs] used to hunt over toward Norman in those mountains and up to Bear Lake. They followed the Mackenzie River to Fort Simpson to get their groceries. [In the era in which this story is set, there were no groceries to get. Only tea and perhaps flour.] There was no fort here then [the first Fort Rae was established in 1852]. There's one place where the river turns [gestures a ninety-degree angle] where it is very narrow with strong rapids and steep banks on both sides. An old fellow who's a great medicine man lived there with three wives, and everybody was scared of him. He's no friend to nobody. Still, they got to pass him there at his fish camp every time they go that way to Simpson. He gives them lunch, fish, and while they're eating he goes out and helps himself to whatever they got in their canoe. Nobody could say a word to him. He done that for years and years, he stays there with his three wives.

One time this Dogrib bunch was going to Great Bear Lake. It was fall. They went to Simpson to get groceries and clothing for winter and then they come back again past that old fellow's place. He was never scared of nobody because he thinks he knows. [The Dogribs said,] "Tomorrow we're going to see that old man, we better watch ourselves, we got families so we better let him help himself." Just before sundown they come to his place and the old man's three wives they cooked for the bunch, and the old man went to the shore, where he helped himself again, taking anything he wants. Gaxieh didn't like that, so to make the old man mad he pick up the youngest wife, grab her, take her out. The woman didn't want to go, but she'd be killed if she didn't. He took her to the bush alongside of the camp. "Boys, make a good fire here," he says, "we're going to have a good time tonight!" The old man returns and says, "What are you doing with that woman?" And Gaxieh says, "What about yourself, what about that stuff you didn't pay for?" The old man says, "I'll give it back, you give me back my wife." Gaxieh says, "Yes, after we're through with her," and they make a fire and everybody help themselves. The old man is burning, he's so mad. All the men with Gaxieh are scared then, they cry and are afraid of a storm. They say, "Maybe something bad will happen." Gaxieh says, "Don't cry, let's go." The men say, "You're a bad man, you shouldn't have done that. That old man is a troublemaker, something is going to happen."

Finally they get to Bear Lake and they're going to cross it. That's a pretty big lake. Before he gets into his canoe, Gaxieh breaks off three little willows and puts them in his canoe and then he follows the rest. He's going to use the willows to kill the wind. So halfway across Bear Lake the men see a little black cloud up in the sky. They all start to yell, "Hey, hey, we told you something was going to happen!" They're all in birchbark canoes. They see a black wall of storm coming and the water is flying and they all cry, "We're never going to see our family and kids. It's your fault!" And Gaxieh says, "Let me go on ahead." So he goes on ahead. When the wind hits the canoes he just gives one whack on the water with the willow and the wind drops dead. "You fellows go on ahead." He's got one willow gone. He knows three kind of wind but other fellows know only one. When they're getting close to shore, Gaxieh yells at them, "Hurry up, hurry up, because this wind I'm sitting on is trying to get up!" As soon as they all hit the shore he stands up and Whoooo, all black water! And that's how he saved their lives.

The old man got something in his mind yet. Gaxieh was not married but finally he married a Bear Lake girl and his brother-in-law, his mother-in-law, his father-in-law, and his sister-in-law, gee whiz, they all like him because he's good hunter. So they all watch him. So one morning all the others were in bed and he went for shooting ducks by himself. The old man was still after Gaxieh and he turned into a big jackfish. Gaxieh was shooting black ducks, not watching the canoe, and all of a sudden he seen a big fish come up under the canoe. It upset the canoe and it all busted and nobody in the camp woke up. So the young fellow turns himself into a loon and he was just calling "ow, ow, ow, ow" back and forth in front of the camp. When his father-in-law got up and he finds his son-in-law is missing he wakes the family. "Must be something happened because that loon has been traveling back and forth calling. Go hunt for him." So the brothers-in-law go hunt for him and finally they find an empty canoe and the loon is following them. When they find the canoe and it's busted in two halves too and they seen that loon following, they knew it means something. They said, "What can we do to save your life? You turned into a loon." Gaxieh says, "Give me clothes so I can turn into a man again." So his brother-in-law just throws his coat to that loon and Gaxieh goes to shore and he turns into a man again. So his brothers-in-law make a new birchbark canoe for him. Didn't take any time, in three days they make him a canoe.

Gaxieh says, "If I don't stop him, that old man, he'll keep on doing it, so I'll see him tonight." But the others say, "Don't try, he's too strong." Gaxieh says, "If I don't, he'll clean everybody, might as well go." Everybody goes to bed and Gaxieh travels, sort of flies—took an airplane I guess! [Vital laughs.] He went to the old man's camp and there's a tree by the shore there. Gaxieh went right into that tree and he watched when that old man wake up.

The old man wakes up and goes to his canoe to go out and visit his net. Right there on the road [trail] where he comes up from his canoe is another tree, two trees, and so Gaxieh set a snare for him there. Gaxieh says [to himself], "If he knows snares, he'll save his life, but if he don't know, too bad for him." That old man came up and went right into that snare, he had that snare on his throat.

Gaxieh went right home that same night. His body was there sleeping all night but his *ink'on* went away and when his *ink'on* come back he wakes up. He says, "I wonder what news we hear from there next time.

I think I got him." Next time they hear that that old man came back from his nets and just drop dead. That's all they know.

Gaxieh means 'Packing Rabbits'. I forget the old man's name.

Gaxieh's father was Edzagwo [a Dogrib culture hero] . . . He was the bravest fellow of the Dogrib and Bear Lake bands. Edzagwo's number one wife was Loche Tail and Edzagwo's oldest son was Edzo. [For more on Edzo, see below]. Edzagwo had twelve wives and when he comes back from hunting all those kids run out to meet him crying, *"Etah! Etah! Etah! Etah!"* ['Papa'].

[Q] A man can turn himself into whatever thing his *ink'on* is.

Alphonse Turns into a Wolf

Nagan are often described in the ethnographic literature on the Dene as mysterious bush dwellers and prowlers (MacNeish 1954; Basso 1978). Vital seemed to equate them to rather matter-of-fact, if vague, enemies (nat'in) *like the Crees and Chipewyans of yore (Helm and Gillespie 1981).*

David W his father, Alphonse, went hunting once in the summer and shot two, three caribou on a point where he was all by himself. He just began to butcher them and he never notice nothing. All of a sudden he hears something and looks up and there's a bunch of *nagan* there. That band try to cover him, to move around him, to catch him, and he runs for the water. They thought he wouldn't go in the water but when he got there he just walked on the water. They rushed at him and he dived under, so they waited. They waited for him surely to come up soon, and they wait with guns for him to come out. Then, about a half mile across, they saw a wolf come out of the water and go into the bush.

That David (b. 1903) is a great medicine man too, they say, because his father is one. But he never tells, they never do, just like he's in hiding. He can cure people but I don't know if he can change himself into something.

Ts'ocia

Ts'ocia, the blind medicine man, died last winter [of 1972–73]. [Q] His spirit goes with the north pole. And he could read your mind—a real Dogrib.

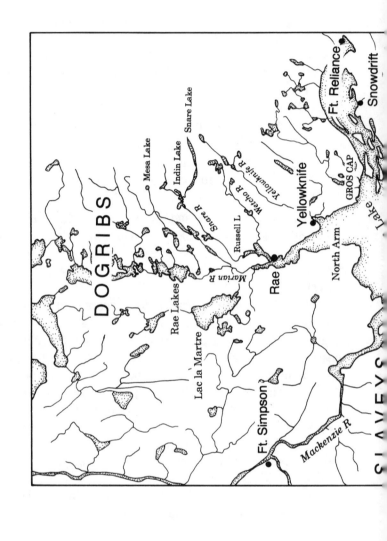

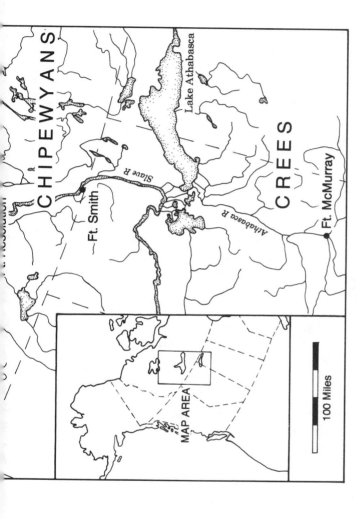

Figure 3. From Great Bear Lake to Fort McMurray: Settlements and Topographic Features Referred to in *Ink'on* Stories.

Godeh and the York Boat Brigade, 1962 Version

We were talking about York boats, the Hudson's Bay Company's cargo carriers in the nineteenth-century fur trade. Vital described them as "heavy as a schooner and about the same size, but with no cabin. Usually there were sixteen oars, eight men on each side, but sometimes twelve oars, six men each side." From 1852 to the 1880s, from old Fort Rae the Company's York boat carried the winter's take of fur across Great Slave Lake then up the Slave River, across the sixteen-mile portage at Fort Smith and on to Fort McMurray on the Athabasca River, the transshipment point for furs out of the north and trade goods in (see fig. 3). On the rivers where the water was swift the crew tracked (towed by hand line) the boat upstream. On their return the Dogrib crew had to first take the York boat to Simpson to get paid, and only then they returned to Fort Rae.

The York boat would leave here when the ice leaves in early June and come back 'way in September. A man got paid one hundred skins [Made Beaver, the Hudson's Bay Company's unit of trade] for all summer. They got to track [upstream] the York boat from Simpson to Great Slave Lake. Sometimes [on the trip back from Simpson] they freeze in and walk back. They would put the supplies [trade goods] in a cache to be hauled by dogs. Each tribe [each fort] had its own York boat. Twelve, fourteen York boats would all come together at the Fort Smith portage. The Dogribs always beat everybody for rowing and portaging. They tried to see how much and how fast they can tackle the portage. Old Henry Lafferty [a métis] used to say, "Nobody can beat us Dogribs."

One man from down river [the Mackenzie], I don't know where he come from, was a great medicine man. He was on top of all the Dogribs and Crees, no one could beat him. Sometimes the men would get so tired rowing they'd ask the old man, "Could you give us a rest? If we could sail on this lake, it would give us a chance for rest." "Well now, if you fellows want a rest I'll see what I can do." And he starts to sing and [Vital gestures] hits the side of the boat, "Put the sail up! Take a good rest." And it don't matter if the wind's not blowing, the sail [and the boat] keeps on going.

And when they come to enemies—like Crees, strangers, they're wicked, them guys—as long as that man is with them they are safe. One time coming downstream [probably on the Athabasca River, in Cree country] the Crees were waiting at a bend of the river with guns. So, when they come past the point at swift rapids, there the Crees are waiting with guns and arrows to kill the men and get stuff for nothing. The Indians

Dogribs in York boat under sail. "Sometimes the men would get so tired rowing they'd ask the old man, 'Could you give us a rest?' ... And it don't matter if the wind's not blowing, the sail [and the boat] keeps on going." Nearing Fort Rae, Great Slave Lake, 1913. Photo by J. A. Mason, National Museum of Canada.

knew about it two days ahead, some guys are pretty smart. The medicine man says, "I'll be on the first boat so they can't do nothing." There's a line of York boats—the medicine man is on the first boat. The medicine man says, "Go right into them. I'll jump out and shake hands with them, and no one will move." So he did that. He jumped out, shook hands with one man, and he says, "Everything is okay now." And the Crees just drop their guns, changed their mind. He shake hands with them so they could change their mind. And all the York boats passed through. Sure saved lots of souls, that guy. And the traders too liked him—long as they got him, they had no trouble. And the medicine men were jealous of him, but couldn't do nothing. They try to kill him, but he know it and they can't do nothing. His son is still alive, pretty old, down at Simpson. [The next day Vital recalled the man's name: Godeh. Is it *Gaudet,* a métis name long associated with the Hudson's Bay Company at Good Hope?]

In the 1880s steamboats replaced York boats in the fur trade on the Athabasca and Mackenzie rivers. York boats continued in use in transportation between Fort Rae (by 1906, New Fort Rae) and Fort Resolution on Great Slave Lake into the second decade of the twentieth century.

Godeh and the York Boat Brigade, 1969 Version

In this account Vital's count of seven major forts is probably correct. I reckon Fort McPherson (rather than Aklavik, which was not yet in existence) for the Loucheux (Gwich'in), Fort Good Hope for the Hare Indians, Fort Norman for the Bearlake Dene and Mountain Dene, Fort Simpson and Fort Providence for the Slaveys, Fort Rae for the Dogribs, and Fort Resolution for the Chipewyans.

At McMurray, lots of fun. Lots of people [York boat crews] from Aklavik, Simpson, Providence, Good Hope—seven forts. My grandfather says that every time we [Dogribs] go for a race with rowers, we beat them. For packing on the portages too, the Dogribs win. On the way back, they get to [Great] Slave Lake but they got to go to Simpson with the York boat with the freight and all, in order to get paid. After they are paid, they got to go back [upstream on the Mackenzie] to Slave Lake, dragging that boat, pull, pull, pull, days after days. By the time they get back, it's the end of September.

Amongst all of the people—Bearlake Indians, Loucheux, Hare, Slavey, Dogribs, Chipewyans—one man is the strongest for *ink'on.* His name was Godeh. No one could beat him. He was one of the strongest medicine men. That's the man my grandfather used to tell about. When it was calm and the men were tired of rowing, they'd say, "Godeh, we'd like to have a real smoke, can you help us for sail?" "Okay boys, fill your pipes," and he'd hit the drum with his hand and sing. And they put up a big sail and they start to sail.

And one time he save lots of peoples' lives. Because the Crees got beat for rowing and packing portage they got jealous. They brought the news back to other Crees and they all got mad. We heard they were waiting for us at a narrows, going to kill us with guns.

We got to pass through there, all the York boats coming. So they told Godeh, "That's going to be a dangerous place. Can you help us?" "Okay, I'll go in the lead." So he's standing right at the [front] end of the York boats and the Crees are all standing with their guns. "We'll go into them. You wait in the boat and I'll run around the camp."

The Crees had muzzle-loaders. Godeh told the pilot to hit the shore. The pilot was scared. Godeh: "Go in! Go in! Once I jump out I don't think they'll do anything." He start to run amongst the Crees—making friends with the women and the men—and they don't say a word. And then Godeh run back to the York boats: "Let's go!" So the Crees stand 'til the last boat pass. Godeh: "I don't think they got no members [memory]," Seven York boats and Godeh saved them.

So every time they go in the York boats they take Godeh with them. With Godeh, they are safe among strangers. And some jealous guys try to kill Godeh with medicine. But they can't. Finally he was so old he couldn't hardly travel. He went hunting with his son and came to a portage, following his son. There's a dead log. He caught his foot on a little branch and fell and died. [Q] Yes, my grandfather knew him.

Another Story about Calling up the Wind

We were in a bay, way across, cutting wood. Eight men were in a crew cutting for the Bay, eight men working for the mission, eight men working for NT [Northern Traders], and eight for Lamson Hubbard. Each crew of men was making a raft. You got to pole it. So four men on each side [of each raft], poling, and it takes a whole day to push the raft from that bay to here. There were fifteen or twenty cords in one raft. Gee whiz, we're tired. And one young fellow, he was a medicine man. We were just ready to go. We ask him to make wind. So we give him one niggerhead twist [tobacco]. And across the little bay, about a hundred feet, there was a bunch making a raft. And a fellow there says, "Shit! That man's not worth nothing. He can't make wind. He's got no power." The medicine man says, "Who, me? I'll show you!" He tells us to put up a sail pole. We do and put up a tent for a sail. And he starts to yell and he throws his cap in the water: "Here the wind starts to come!" We could see a little cloud on the west side and then a breeze start and then it blows worse and worse. It was no trouble to come home. And he says, "I'm a medicine man now!"

How the *Ink'on* Got the Manager's Mind

This story was first published under the joint authorship of Helm and Thomas (1966). Eleven years later it appeared in a collection of American Indian stories, where it was accompanied by a very brief but error-riddled introduction. I had the opportunity, face-to-face, to stress to the compiler the grievous flaws in that introduction and to offer to provide the corrections. I now find (1991) the same introduction to Vital's story (retitled "The Bewitched Pale Man") repeated in an expanded collection, Native American Testimony, *by the same editor. So I am here seizing the chance to nail the plethora of misinformation lodged in that introduction:*

> *Because the Dogrib of Canada* had to cross the terrain [wrong] *of* their greatest enemy, the Maskegon Indians [wrong], in order to trade with the French [wrong], *they conducted their business with the Hudson's Bay Company* instead [misleading]. *This tale was recited by Vital Thomas, a contemporary Dogrib storyteller from* Rae, near Marten Lake [wrong], *in* central Canada [wrong]. *[Nabokov 1991:47]*

Dogribs used to go to Simpson to trade. It's an old fort. They'd go to Simpson in the fall from here. One bunch went on ahead of the other by four or five days. They got to Simpson and the Hudson's Bay manager was mad at them. He wouldn't give them any credit. He said, "You guys haven't paid me from last year. I won't give you a thing." Poor Indians, nothing they could do but go back. Pretty soon they meet the other bunch coming along, the day before the other bunch would reach the fort. They said to the other bunch, "No use going on, you might as well turn back. Manager won't give us credit. Nothing there for you."

There was an old fellow with them, Seretton's father—not that Seretton Football, now, another one—and he heard the talking and he said, "Well, we might as well go in and see what it's like. Got to go anyway, can't turn back now." So they kept on going and got to the fort tomorrow [next day]. Those fellows ask the old man if he could change the manager's mind, they'd come from a long ways, Snare Lake or Indin Lake. They pay the old man and he says, "I'll do the best I can to change his mind." He starts singing and then he puts his arms down in the earth, in the mud about half way up [gestures to elbows] and he's singing, "Hey, hey, Pale Man! Here is the man you talk about," and he brought the Hudson's Bay man up out of the ground, brought up just his head and to here [gestures mid-chest] and he rubs his hands [Vital gestures as if over the manager's head, like pulling or cupping up water and then claps his hands together loudly] and says, "Here it is! I got his mind in my hand. He's gone home now without his mind. As soon as we get there we got to go right back, I can't hold his mind very long."

They start out early and get there about the middle of the day and they ask for everything and that manager is like he's half drunk. Give, give all the men ask him for. Then the old man says, "Might as well go home now, I can't hold it any longer." That man [manager] was like dreaming, like he's asleep. When they got to the bush he sent back his mind.

Afterwards, Simpson fellows [Slaveys] say to them, "After you guys left that manager is sure mad. He says its like he just wake up. 'I don't know why I gave them all those things. I wouldn't give the first bunch any credit'. If they didn't have that old man with them they couldn't do it.

The same ink'on *"technique" of capturing an adversary's mind or spirit is featured in Naidzo's story of Edzo and Akaitcho, in chapter 7.*

Got'ocia

At Lac la Martre, before Treaty came, there was one fellow making medicine because there was a sick man. And the medicine man wanted a woman to come, he wanted to ask her how the sickness started. He sent for her and she refused to come. And the medicine man was singing, "I want her to come. I want to ask her questions. Maybe this man was sick on account of that woman." So the medicine man sent for her again and she wouldn't come. Twice he send for her.

"If she don't want to come, I'll make her come." In them days, they had eagle feathers for their bows and arrows. So the medicine man calls for an eagle feather. "If she don't want to come, this will take her." And he put the eagle feather upright, stuck in the floor. And he start to sing to the feather and the woman run to beat hell inside [the dwelling where the medicine men is]. And the medicine man says, "You're not the boss. As long as this feather is here, I'm boss."

The medicine man's name was Got'ocia—Our Tits' Little Brother. Maybe his mother or father call him that name when he was a little kid.

I think it was the same fellow—no, it was his father. He [the father] lost his wife. He took his two little boys with him to hunt. They were alone in the bush. The kids were crying because their moccasins were torn, they couldn't travel. It was summer.

The father shot a moose and fries the meat. There is nobody to clean the moosehide and his boys are crying because their moccasins are torn. And the man says, "One time I saw a man shake a hide [Vital acts it out] and on the first shake all the hair fell out. And on the second shake the hide was tanned. And on the third shake the hide was smoked."

And the man did it. On the first shake all the hair fell out and on the second shake it was tanned and on the third it was turning brown. That's how he fixed the hide and started to make moccasins for his boys.

That was just the spirit [that tanned the hide]. They [men with *ink'on*] could do anything. But with bad fellows, you got to be careful with them, even till now. If one don't like you, if you don't keep your word, he might send medicine to make you crippled or lame. Those kind of medicine men you shouldn't laugh at them. Joke with them is all right, but to make them worried is no good.

Bad Medicine: Old Marrow

Old Marrow [pseudonym] sure killed lots of fellows. He don't do it with his hand, he just does it in hiding, puts his mind to it, you can't prove it. [Why?] Somebody might say something he don't like and he says, "Some day you'll find out if I'm good [powerful] or not, after you leave." Maybe it's winter and next summer the fellow will be crippled or something. He waits until the fellow forgets about it. [Q] Yes, a man who killed could cure too but didn't cure much, his mind is just for killing. A good doctor don't bother nobody. Got a strong mind.

[Q] Yes, if somebody is sick from one *ink'on* another *ink'on* can cure him if he is better than the one who made him sick. If you don't know about *ink'on*, *ink'on* can't hurt you. Mostly *ink'ons* go after each other, they are jealous of each other. But if a fellow wants to make love to a girl, an *ink'on* can make her follow him. [Q] Crees chew things, here [we Dogribs] just think, got a strong mind. No roots and stuff. We don't show nothing. Crees got roots, plants.

Several years after Vital's account of Old Marrow, Alphonse Eronchi provided a different slant:

Old Marrow was a medicine man. But he can't do on [cure] any human because he claimed his medicine was bad.

He was a kid, hunting in the bush, and the enemy was chasing him. When the enemy got close, he shot the enemy through the heart. He became sick because he had killed a person. If you kill a person, you got to taste the blood, cut [the person, apparently] into pieces, and sing. He didn't have time to do that. Because he was unable to do that, his medicine would kill a human being. So he could never cure. But he was a great hunter [due to the strength of his medicine].

At another time, Vital commented that Old Marrow was "one of the strongest medicine men in Rae" and that he was the first to die in the

Old Beaverhook's widow, Madelaine. Lac la Martre, 1959.

1928 flu epidemic. Apparently Joseph Marrow, the failed prophet, was his son.

The Crippling of Beaverhook

Old Beaverhook [of Marten Lake, dead for a number of years] didn't always used to be crippled. It happened just before he married his second wife. Somebody was jealous of him [because] he could walk so fast. When they fight [raced] on snowshoes he always gets there first. He never stop for tea when he goes to the fort, just keeps on going, others can't keep up. Somebody made medicine to make him crippled. They use their minds and take the marrow out of a man's bones. Legs are no good if the marrow is gone, can't walk. They do that to animals too, [those] hunting caribou, those *ink'on*, can take the marrow out of the bones and the caribou can't go farther.

Unintended Harm from Medicine

Old Beaverhook's second wife's grandchild died after Beaverhook died. That man was *ink'on*. You can't keep nothing from a dead man. If an *ink'on* dies and maybe he's had his little grandchild with him a lot and left some medicine, after a while the child will die too.

7

Ink'on in Play and Legend

Ink'on in the Hand Game

Except for the last story, this section is taken, with a few adjustments, from the report by Helm and Lurie (1966) on the Dogrib hand game. All three stories of ink'on *in the hand game are from Vital Thomas.*

The Dogrib hand game is a fast-tempo guessing game played to the accompaniment of vigorous drumbeats and chanting. There are two teams. The players of each team arrange themselves in a single line along one side of a tent to face the opponents on the other side. Throughout the game, players of both teams maintain the characteristic kneeling-seated posture of the Indian man.

One team at a time operates as the active playing team. Each playing member of that team hides a token (idzi) in one of his fists. A single member of the opposing team serves as the guesser, who by means of a hand signal guesses simultaneously against all the opposing men, indicating in which fist each man holds his idzi. It is the objective of the guesser in each guess to "kill" as many of the opponents as possible by correctly guessing the disposition of the concealed tokens. Once all opposing players are killed, the right to be the playing (hiding) team passes to the other side.

It is the playing team that scores. For every man who is missed on each guess, the playing team receives one tally stick. If the playing team can accumulate all the tally sticks twice in succession, the men of this team have won a game and will be paid individually by opposing bettors on the opposite team. The function of the guesser of the nonplaying team is to eliminate as quickly as possible all the players of the active team so that the right to be the active hiding team, and therefore scoring team, may

121

The Old Chief as guesser in the hand game with his "team" of Edge-of-the-Woods men.
The man in the white shirt is the great-grandson of the Snare Prophet. Rae, 1962.

again return to his side. Only by being in action as the playing team can
a team hope to win games.

Taiya and the Bear Lake Man

In the old days there were great medicine men for *idzi*. The Bear Lake
Indians and the Dogribs used to play the hand game. The Bear Lake
Indians had one head man for *idzi*, and there was Taiya, the Dogrib, who
was a great man—he knew something about *idzi*. The Dogribs were
playing the Bear Lake Indians. The Dogribs had been losing for two days
and they said to one another, "There is only one man that counts in that
Bear Lake bunch." Finally they told Old Man Taiya to be guesser for *idzi*
[to counteract the powerful Bear Lake man]. Taiya agreed, "I'll be
guesser." So he starts to guess and every time he guesses he kills every
man except that old man, that Bear Lake man who knows something
about *idzi*.

So suppose [as was the case in this game] that there is one old man left
who knows something about *idzi*. The guesser is going to tell him, "*ne*
re si 'ah"—'I'm going to have a good guess'. It also means 'I'll try my
best'. And the old man that he is guessing against [the Bear Lake man]
holds his hands out and he shakes them at the guesser, showing *idzi* in one

hand, shaking both his hands in front of the guesser's face [hands open and palms up to show his *idzi*] and saying, "I got this. Come on if you are good enough!" That Bear Lake man had a bear tooth in his hand. He had been using it all along for *idzi*. [After the Bear Lake man had doubled over, shuffled his *idzi*, and straightened up awaiting the bet] Taiya went like this: [CLAP!]. And the Bear Lake man fell on his back, unconscious, with a broken arm. The arm of the hand that held the bear tooth was broken. The Bear Lake man thought he knew something, but the Dogrib man knew more about *idzi*. The Dogribs won back all they had lost and finally the Bear Lake Indians lost too much so they quit playing. You can't do anything unless you know about *idzi*.

One Foot in Heaven's Father and the Bear Lake Chief

The Dogribs never get beat much for medicine men. There was a Bear Lake man who was *denekawi* [trading chief] for the Bear Lakers. He was called Slim Ekawi. He was a big, tall man. He was supposed to be a great medicine man and a good hunter so he was on top of [greater than] a *k'awo* [boss or ordinary leader].

So one time the Bear Lake Indians came into Rae. The Hudson's Bay store knew him so that they counted him for [treated him as] *denekawi*. He always carried a knife on his side at about his waist, held with a string that went over his head and one shoulder. The Bear Lake Indians and the Dogribs were playing the hand game, and the Bear Lake Indians were winning because their *denekawi* knew everything about *idzi*. The *et'at'in* [regional band] had joined the Bear Lake bunch and the Dogribs were losing. One Foot in Heaven was a poor trapper but a great medicine man. He was one of the best doctors to cure and One Foot in Heaven he too knew everything about *idzi*. So he started to play on the Dogrib side and he had something in his hand out of medicine, so he is going to win [or so he thinks]. And One Foot in Heaven's father, an old man, he was standing in the door of the tipi, watching. That man was number one man for medicine. No one can beat him. He was watching his son playing.

So the Bear Lake *denekawi* was going to guess. Now, if a man doesn't know much about the game he will get killed. So One Foot in Heaven's father was watching. He knew that the Bear Lake Chief was going to play tricks on his boy. He knew what was going on. As soon as the Bear Lake *denekawi* clapped, One Foot in Heaven dropped back. If his father hadn't been there, his son would be dead, because as soon as the Bear Lake Chief clapped and One Foot in Heaven dropped back, his father grabbed at the air and he had his son's *idzi* in his hand.

And the father says, "You guys from Bear Lake always make trouble. If I was young, I would be in that game. But as long as I am here you won't do any tricks like that." And the *denekawi* from Bear Lake was scared, because he knew there was someone better than he was.

If that old man had not been there, One Foot in Heaven would be in heaven! [Laughter] I saw the game . . . it must have been back in 1918, about.

[A discussion of the points in the story with Vital made the course of events somewhat more explicit]. Yes, One Foot in Heaven's father grabbed through the air [magically for his son's *idzi*]. If he hadn't grabbed it, his son would be dead. If the old man had missed *idzi*, *idzi* could have gone some place with a power in it and could have killed One Foot in Heaven. But the old man grabbed it and stopped it.

Otendah

The study of the hand game was based on data gathered in the 1962 field season. In the resulting publication we stated that "no attribution of 'medicine for idzi' is made of men living today" (Helm and Lurie 1966:85). But when we returned to Rae in 1967 we got the following account from Vital.

In Yellowknife now there is a young man twenty-five or twenty-six years old whose name is Otendah. That means "Eskimo." You can't play with him. Every time he plays hands no one else can win. It's like he knows what is in your [the guesser's] mind, what way you are going to point [i.e., which of his fists the guesser will indicate as the one that holds the token]. Sometimes he gets ashamed of himself and just kills himself [i.e., deliberately allows the guesser to guess the correct hand.] He was here last summer and he was winning, winning, winning three games in a row. So everyone quit playing. He came again at Christmas, and the people told him "Next time if you're going to play we won't," because he was winning again. [Question: Does he have power or know about other powerful things?] He should.

"Playing" with *Ink'on*

During our joint 1962 field period Nancy Lurie went to Lac la Martre, and I stayed in Rae, using for the first time a key informant, Vital Thomas. Every time a pontoon plane flew between Rae and Lac la Martre, Lurie and I sent each other messages and carbon copies of field notes. One packet from Lurie contained accounts of two "games" that were in years past *"played" at Lac la Martre:* dzekwin *and* tsinco *[as pronounced by Vital; Nancy obtained three other idiolects for the words].*

Dzekwin

I ask Vital about "wearing a mask and playing." He knows at once what I am referring to.

Some kind of animal, like a human, shows itself in the bush. And if you know that fellow *[dzekwin]*, you will be a good hunter, the luckiest man. [Q] You put birchbark on your face and make a nose, heavy eyebrows, red cheeks, and little whiskers [Vital gestures to indicate chin whiskers about four inches long]. And you put spruce boughs in your back so it is like a humpback and you carry a little axe.

Father Amourous played in that game. We had that game about two years ago. John Beaulieu was the one. He is sure good, because when he was a little kid he sees that *[dzekwin]* and he *[dzekwin]* tells you how often you should play.

[Q] Just one fellow plays. [Q] Yes, he makes a mask of birchbark. [Q] Nobody has a mask like that around here because you make the mask just for the game, when you are asked to play. You throw the mask away afterwards.

Father Amourous didn't believe it. We had just stopped at the narrows at Russell Lake. There was a whole bunch from Russell Lake and a bunch from Marian River, and they stop there a couple of weeks before they come into Rae.

"Let's play *dzekwin!*" Can't choose just any man because he [just any man] don't know. You must find a man that does know, and he'll draw his face and there's lots of fun. You can only play in the spring, May and part of June. You can't play in fall or winter or summer. In the olden days, every spring they played.

The next day we took up the topic of dzekwin *again and we establish that both the man "playing" and the* dzekwin-*being are called* dzekwin.

If we want to ask man to play, we say "Let's play *dzekwin!*" If he [the individual who met *dzekwin* as a boy] don't do what *dzekwin* tells him to do, when he gets older he's going to have bad luck or something. [Q] Some other guys besides John Beaulieu know how to play, but John was the man who played it last time, last summer. In old days, they used to play almost every spring. That game, it's pretty near the end of it [it is dying out].

At the start, they got to dress him [the *dzekwin* enactor] up, 'way in a corner of the bush. Two fellows who know about *dzekwin* got to dress this man—with a mask and spruce boughs so he looks like a hunchback. And fifty, sixty people are all waiting in line. And *dzekwin* carries an axe [held up at shoulder height] and he goes like this [indicates a jogging step and movement of shoulders as *dzekwin* looks first to one side, then the other]. And *dzekwin* looks all through the bush, like he is looking for caribou. And when he sees all the fellows in one line, *dzekwin* has a great big pile of spruce boughs in one hand and he give one little bough to each man in the line. When he is through, he has given a bough to every man in the bush, and when he gets to end of line he turns back to the bush. And they all throw their boughs at him and say to him, "Grandfather, your meat stinks!"— *"ehtse, nindih mah!"* When he gives the spruce boughs to the men, that means he is giving food to us. So when he hears that ["your meat stinks"] he gets mad and starts to chase all the fellows with the axe. Chase, chase and if he grabs somebody he'll sit on his arse and start to hit the ground with his axe. He's glad because he thinks it's [the man is] a caribou. And another fellow will say, "Grandfather, that caribou stinks. It's no good." And *dzekwin* jumps up, looks around [Vital imitates back and forth swiveling of head], and he starts to chase that fellow. He don't say a word. Anything we tell him, he believe it.

If he catch a person, that person got to fall like this [Vital indicates face down], and *dzekwin* sits on his arse. [The description from Lac la Martre implies that *dzekwin* pretends to defecate or do something "dirty" on the man]. *Dzekwin* chops on each side of him with the axe, just like he's going to butcher the man. Before he [actually] does that, another man tells him "That caribou stinks, it's been dead so long!" And *dzekwin* jump up and start to chase another man the first way he runs.

You should come early in the spring [to see *dzekwin*]. [Q] They'll play if you ask them. Father Amourous didn't believe about that. He went with us and saw it. You can't play *dzekwin* in camp, not supposed to play in camp. Got to be out in the bush. And no young kids. [Q] Women can watch but they don't play, don't get boughs. The women make a big fire. From there they can watch. As long as they got the fire going, *dzekwin* can't come close. Like an old fellow who can't play, he makes the fire, watches.

Sure smart, them guys, and fast too. [Q] The playing lasts an hour or more.

Usually [to play *dzekwin*] they stop between Marian River and Russell Lake, at the narrows, just before they get to the fort, in the beginning of June. [Q] You just ask them to play, you don't pay because him, too, he is willing to play. But if he don't do what *dzekwin* tells him, he'll get bad luck or something.

In another four or five years, I don't think they will play again. Because these young fellows, they don't care for nothing.

The descriptions of the playing of dzekwin *gained by Lurie at Lac la Martre correspond in basics with Vital Thomas' account. The only possibly significant departure is the lack of designation of the particular* dzekwin-*being as the animating and validating agency for the enactor, the "medicine man." Neither* dzekwin *nor* tsinco *[see below] had been played for several years because at Lac la Martre "the medicine men are dead" and "only the medicine men know how to play." Beaverhook (see entries on him, above), Jeremy Beaulieu, and Chi knew how. Actually, of course, Chi was alive in 1962.*

In early June 1973, shortly before I arrived at Rae, dzekwin *was played, apparently not in the bush but alongside the road, not far from the settlement. In Elizabeth Mackenzie's description, "Three men tried to start but I think something was wrong, they didn't play much. There were too many girls. In the old time teenage girls never go near such a place. If we did, they chased us away right away."*

Vital was also present at the 1973 playing. He named David W (see above) and John Beaulieu as two performers. "But they didn't play long. Too many young guys there, they don't know nothing. There were so many drunks they couldn't play." Vital showed little interest in pursuing the topic of dzekwin, *saying only, "Not many know about it—it's something like* ink'on. Ink'on *tells them when to play. The smart ones they can play good and could cure someone from sickness." This was a facet that neither Lurie at Lac la Martre nor I with Vital had picked up in 1962. But Elizabeth Mackenzie brought up curing as a major theme of* dzekwin—*perhaps it was a particular rationale of the 1973 enactment of* dzekwin:

That kind of game is when you yourself [the enactor] or someone else is sick. Or the person feels like something is going to happen. The person wants to play but he can't say anything. Someone else has to ask him to play and *then* he says yes. You start after midnight and play until three or four in the morning in the fall. [Since *dzekwin* had been enacted about 15 June, only a week before Mrs. Mackenzie's description, it appears she confounded *spring* and *fall* in this account.] Long ago they used to play like that. After they [the *dzekwin* enactor] finish, they got new gloves, new shoes, new axe [gifts], because they play with medicine. They know right away if there is something used, if there are young girls who have used something. And if a young girl gets her monthlies, the person can't play. He just stops and stands very still. Someone knows this and takes his axe and hits at him like medicine, and then he starts again. And when they finish playing, if someone is sick, they bring him to be cured for free. It is only at this time of playing that he can cure for free [without receiving payment-gifts]. He runs after the people and if someone falls, that person won't live long [compare Vital's account of *tsinco,* below].

At the time he is playing he can know of something that will happen next year or next month. He knows very well. He makes a sign [to indicate this knowledge] but he never talks. This was the case with John Pierre playing about 1946 or 1948. We were there. All the people came to a point [on the lake] not far from here. The people from Lac la Martre and Rae Lakes and everybody was there. Maybe a hundred people. They had dancing and the hand game before we came here [to Rae] and they asked John Pierre to play.

He didn't play much. As he was playing he stopped and made a sign with his hands like the sun's rays. [Elizabeth moves her hand, fingers extended, in a semicircle in the air.] He stopped at three o'clock [halfway between horizon and zenith?] and made [gestured] tears down his face.

Next day they were having a hand game. At nine o'clock the news came from across the lake. The players stopped right away. One man was out duck hunting in a canoe and he saw the accident. A young man was putting his shotgun in the canoe and it discharged and shot him in the heart. That young man was the brother of Joe Nascin's wife, Bernadette. So people went to get the police and the boy's father and mother are crying. Bernadette ran away in the bush because she did not like to see her father and mother cry.

Tsinco

Although he had never seen it enacted, Vital knew of tsinco. *He described it in 1962 immediately after his description of* dzekwin.

There is a different game to play. It's got like—what you call it—what the bishop carries? [We agree on the bishop's "staff."] A man's got one like it, a big long pole, and that man, you can't hide nothing from him—button, iron, he'll find it. Maybe fifty years ago [hidden for fifty years] but he'll dig it out. The play is called *tsinco.*

[Q] Just do it for play. Not many alive now, about all gone now [who can do this]. Haven't seen that game for thirty years. But my mother used to tell about it. Last time I heard of that game was at Marten Lake. [Q] Yes a woman can do it too. But not young fellows. And that man [who enacts *tsinco*] will tell you how long you're going to live. It's different from *dzekwin.* Both playing, but different.

The pole is called *tsinco teh.* [Q] A man got to have a spirit to do this. They're all gone now. Just at Marten Lake, Chi is the only one who knows about that. [Q] Got to ask him [the man who enacts *tsinco*] to do it. Or if he wants to play, he has got to tell other fellows: "My spirit tells me pret' near time to play." The news goes all over. The older men say, "If that's the way it is, we got to play."

It don't matter if a man got great medicine. He can't play if he doesn't know *tsinco*. It's like a miracle.

And you got to dress him up. [Q] I don't know how, I have never seen it myself. And he chase some men one way and other men another way. One of the men can take a button [for example], make little hole in ground with his finger, push the button in, and cover it with dirt. And *tsinco* finishes chasing the first men and then he run toward us, like. And we run and just as he passes the button he goes [Vital indicates stopping, then a stabbing motion of the pole toward the ground] and he stops and takes the button out of the ground. He don't pass [go on by] any iron or nothing. It don't matter how long underground [it has been]. It is just like the button [or whatever] sticks to his pole.

But that's a hard game because you got to be careful, because you got to have three or four guys that know about how to play. They got their own way to talk to him. It's a dead game now.

And after they play, all the people join with him and ask him, "How long is this man going to live?" and he start to chase that man. And if *tsinco* can't go any farther, it means the man won't live very long. *Tsinco* makes signs only. But if *tsinco* chases that man a long time, he says by signs, "Going to live long, going to see white hair." But if he can't run, that fellow won't live long. And it is true, too.

[Q] He chases a man or woman, either one. He puts on a special outfit. I never see it. My mother and her brothers used to play when I was in school. There were three or four helpers. They dressed him. They know his spirit. Is easy for him to play because the others know. He's something like a bishop, he's got to have helpers.

Even that stick, some of them they dream about it. [Then, when the man] grows older, he says "Got to have *teh* before I die." (*Teh* is 'stick, cane', like in *seteh laiti?* 'Where is my cane?'). Anything they dream about, they go by.

At Lac la Martre Nancy Lurie could not establish the "purpose" of playing tsinco. *She did, however, gain a description of the costumes from two Marten Lake men who had seen performances by the Marten Lake "medicine men" in the past. In their account: Two men, who must be medicine men, dressed up in hood and caribou hide which had Vs painted*

Adele Pig of Lac la Martre. Lac la Martre, 1959.

on the sides. Their arms and faces were painted red and blackened with charcoal. At least one of these men was called tsinco. *Apropos Vital's reference to "iron" and "buttons" [evidently metal buttons], the Marten Lake medicine men "didn't like tin cans" and they discovered any buried ones. Mrs. Mackenzie confirmed that the "staff" or pole "doesn't like any kind of iron, not even a safety pin or needle," and can locate iron in the ground that no one knows is there. Elizabeth had never seen this "play," she had only heard about it.*

From Adele Pig, an elderly granny of Lac la Martre, via her granddaughter: "The only time the people played those games [both dzekwin *and* tsinco] *was in springtime. They're happy, it's springtime, the animals and everything is back."*

History into Legend

As aspects of Dogrib oral history these stories of ink'on *lead back to documented hostilities between Dogribs and enemies in the 1820s and in the 1780s and thence, by the last story, recede into mythic time.*

Edzo and Akaitcho

*The story of the Dogrib Edzo's confrontation of the enemy Yellowknife Akaitcho (*ekeco *'Big Foot') is the Dogrib national epic. During his visit to Rae during Christmas–New Year of 1969–70, Naidzo the Bear Lake Prophet recounted this familiar story that stems from events of the 1820s. As far as living Dogribs are concerned, the historical Yellowknives, who linguistically were a branch of the Chipewyan Dene, and the Chipewyans in general are encompassed under the single term* tedzont'in. *That term is consistently translated by English-speaking Dogribs as 'Chipewyans', as did Vital in translating Naidzo's narrative (featured in Helm and Gillespie 1981). The portion of immediate interest is that treating of* ink'on:*

In order to put an end to the pillaging and killing of Dogribs by Akaitcho and his band, Edzo, with only four companions, determined to seek out the enemy's camp and confront Akaitcho. The five Dogribs were discovered by one of Akaitcho's followers, who fled to alert Akaitcho and his band.

Then Edzo called on his brother Satl'iweta [Sun Ray's Father] to think about what he knows of *ink'on.* Satl'iweta started to sing and at the same time he thrust his hands and his forearms into the earth about one foot deep. And he pulled out a Chipewyan's head. And he took the Chipewyan's head off and he took out his spirit *[inin]*. He pulled that man part way out of the ground and he took his spirit and then he let him go without his spirit. And Satl'iweta tore the spirit in half and sat on half of it. The other half he let go. But the other half did not go back [to the Chipewyans]. Satl'iweta did this so that the Chipewyans would not have any spirit. He said, "Right now they are coming wild, but once they reach here I don't think they will do any harm." Edzo said, "Thanks! That is what we want."

And then Akaitcho's bunch started to come. There were no end to them. . . . The Chipewyans and the Dogribs were no friends to each other, so they met one another like animals. They were ready for a fight. . . . [After a series of dramatic and threatening exchanges between Edzo and Akaitcho] Edzo turned to the enemy and he spoke so loud that when his voice hit the two trees at this place, it was so strong that the trees' branches leaped up in the air. "You talk nice," he said. "It sounds good. I think I will talk the same as you now." And when the branches flew up in the air, Akaitcho started to weep, he was so frightened. After Akaitcho started to cry, they did not say any more words.

That is the way they made peace. So we are friendly with everyone now. Everywhere you go we are friends. If we had not made peace there would be fighting until now. Now everyone can get a decent sleep. That is good. That is the way it happened.

In 1967, a couple of years before Naidzo's narration, Vital Thomas' version of the epic attributed the ink'on *to Edzo:*

So the Dogribs [all brothers in this version] started to make medicine and Edzo made medicine to take the spirit of the Chipewyan so he won't know how to handle a gun. And Edzo made medicine and pretty soon he grabbed Akaitcho's spirit in his hand [Vital demonstrated by clasping his two hands together]. And Edzo says, "This is what I'm looking for!" And he held out his hand and there's something bright as the moon in it. And Edzo says, "Let Akaitcho come."

In 1979 Vital told the following enriched version with such enjoyment that I gained the impression that he had just recently heard it or had had his memory revivified.

Edzo says to one of his brothers, "You're first." His brother sings [makes medicine] and took a gun and tied it like a rope! So the enemies won't shoot their guns. Then Edzo tells another brother to make medicine. So that brother starts to sing, tries to take the spirit of Akaitcho's bunch. And he holds it up, it's just like half of the moon. He holds it like this . . . [Vital demonstrates, showing thumb and fingertips opposed as if holding a dependent object]. Edzo says, "That's not a full spirit!"

So Edzo starts to sing. Edzo sings and he claps his hands and grabs [something] like the full moon or full sun, and his finger is sticking right through the middle of it [Vital demonstrates].

And Edzo says, "That one's a full one! No one is going to hurt us now!"

So [that way] they get everything ready for the enemy . . .

In 1967 aged Pierre Mantla (b. 1877) seized an opportunity to tell Nancy Lurie, through interpreter Joe Drybones, the saga of Edzo. As in Naidzo's account, in Pierre's version Edzo relies solely on his oratory to cow Akaitcho and his followers.

Edzo and the three men with him started to make *ink'on*. The first man's *ink'on* was a black raven. The man said, "If I'm going to die I'll see some dark smoke." So this man turned himself into a black raven and he flew around Akaitcho's camp. But he didn't see any black smoke and so he said, "It's okay for me." The second man said, "When I was young I was told I could go around with the moon. When I die the moon will be half black." So he went around Akaitcho's camp with the moon but nothing happened, the moon was just round and bright. The third man, who was Edzo's brother-in-law, said, "Since I was born, no knife or gun can hurt me. I will live until I die." Then Edzo's brother-in-law said to Edzo, "How are you yourself?" Edzo answered, "I'm not an *ink'on* man, but I can talk. When I was young someone put something on my tongue to talk. I can help myself and help the people."

Massacre at Mbešoti

One of the biggest bands of [Dogrib] Indians got killed at Shoti Lake on Marian River. The place is called Mbešoti. They were killed because the poor Indians made a mistake. Mbešoti is right on Marian River, not too far, two portages from Marian River Village, at a point. All the Indians that summer or spring came into the same camp. There were many people. They would have liked to have fun, but they were scared of Akaitcho. So they put their tipis right out on the point and made a fence right at the back so the enemies could not go over.

They thought that Akaitcho would come by land. But Akaitcho's bunch came by canoe. They had cleaned the Indians at Lac La Martre and were on their way back when they find this big camp. They killed all the Indians. That's when Akaitcho had muzzle-loaders, I think. Some young guys were on an island, to keep away from the camp. [This may be a reference to the practice in "olden times," according to Vital, of segregating pubescent boys on a platform in the bush to help them get *ink'on*.] Some of them changed into otters, but Akaitcho's bunch were shooting and killed them all. They cleaned this biggest camp. That point now is covered with big trees, you couldn't know where the camp was. That was over a hundred years ago, before the white man comes to Rae.

There was one man who had a big family. His name was Egat'o. He went to Marian Lake to get birchbark to make a canoe and when he had enough birchbark he came back home. He didn't know the enemies had cleaned his place. Just before he got to the portage he sees the enemies coming in birchbark canoes that hold eight or nine. There were two or three canoes like that. He turns back and they start to chase him. They chase and chase and finally he went around a corner and they pass him. So they left that guy missing. They were holding their paddles straight up in front of them. [Vital illustrates.] They were so glad that they clean everybody.

That man was a medicine man. He knew something about thunder, so he calls his dream and he can see a little cloud above the enemy. The thunder cracked and upsets all of the canoes and kills all the bunch. Nothing is left but broken canoes and paddles. That's one man who clean the whole bunch.

How the Chipewyans Killed the Bull in the Rock

Under the water in some lakes there are big animals. And some of the same kind of big animals live in certain rocks. One time, the Chipewyans had killed so many Bear Lake and Dogrib Indians. The Bear Lake and Dogrib Indians got mad. They said, "Let's see if we can send starvation to them." So they sent starvation against the Chipewyans. And the Chipewyans couldn't find anything to eat. The caribou were all gone, no sign, and no fish. And the Chipewyans were dying [as they were] going home. Finally, only three or four or five Chipewyans were still alive. They got to a lake where they knew a big bull was in the rock there. And they were so hungry one said, "The only way to save our lives is to kill the bull in the rock." So they put a string around the mountain and they tied all kind of feathers to it—ptarmigan, prairie chicken, duck, eagle, hawk. They tied all the feathers right close together around the big, high rock. And one man starts to make medicine to the string of feathers and the birds come alive, all kinds, to make noise to wake the bull. And the mountain start to shake, it's the bull getting up. And just before the rock cracks one man says, "I'll shoot before he shows himself." So he shot right at the rock and breaks it open and shoots the bull right in the head.

And they cut it up and ate it and saved their lives. About one hundred starved but three made it.

[Q] *nde oye ndih* 'bull'. Some live underwater and some live in mountains. [Q] It's a big animal, but no hair. [Q] Never see it myself. But suppose you are going to the barrens, they'll tell you the places where the bull is. You got to circle way around it, keep away from it.

The Dragon in the Rock

Elizabeth Mackenzie and I were talking about Edzo and this reminded her of the route to the lake, gotsunkati, *where Edzo and Akaitcho made peace. The tale that emerged turned out to be a variant of Vital's story of the "bull" in the rock.*

There is a place on the way to *gotsunkati* where two men made strong medicine. The mark is still on the rock. We went there when I was small and I saw this big rock. [Elizabeth illustrates by placing one condensed milk can on top of another and placing a larger sugar bowl on top.] There were three rocks all together and one stood on top of the other. That is where the two men made strong medicine. They wanted to kill something, something like a dragon, that lived under the big rock. They were very hungry and had nothing to eat so they made strong medicine. Before they made the medicine they talked to each other back and forth just like they were having a meeting [they debated what to do?]

Then one of the men put a hook in a small lake nearby. First on his hook he got an otter. And then he got all kinds of ducks. He got the big duck with the white breast and the black tail that we call *titso* ['loon']. He hooked that too. And he hooked a mink and he hooked all kinds of things. Then he took each of these animals and tied each body on a string so that they hung all around the mountain [the three-part rock.] This was to kill the thing that lived in the rock. Then he [or they] made medicine and started to sing. All of those animal bodies started to shake and shake and cry and cry. He wanted to make a noise big enough. The things cried, cried. And he sings and a big dragon came out because he heard the noise. And then the Indian put a shell in his mouth to make the shell strong. They shoot all together.

The dragon heard all this crying of animals and he came out of a lake nearby. That lake is called *dek'woti* ['Yellow Lake']. It is called that because the water is red or yellow. It still looks like blood. I think those Indians were Chipewyans. They were hungry. I think that those Indians that travel a long way from home must be strong with medicine.

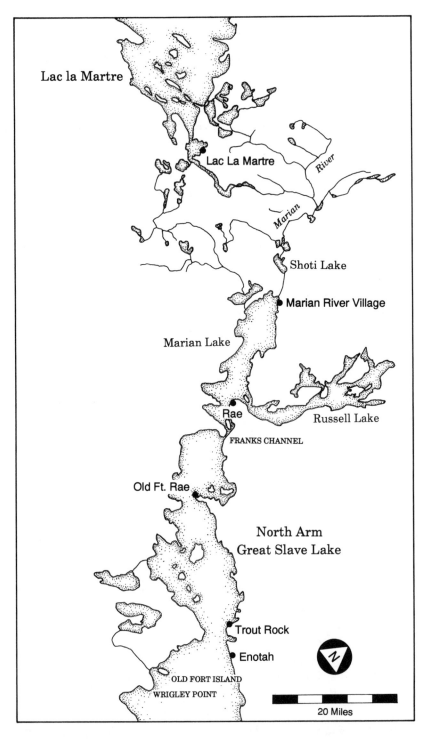

Figure 4. From Lac la Martre to Wrigley Point: Places Featured in *Ink'on* Stories.

Flyman

Figure 4 locates places featured in this story and the following one.

Enotah is a place near Trout Rock [on the North Arm of Great Slave Lake] where people fish now. Across [the North Arm] from Enotah there is a place, it's old-time name was *kwenageh* 'rock rolling' [on the modern map it is Wrigley Point]. The trout at Lac la Martre are good but not as good as at *kwenageh*. This was the first fish camp that we know for thousands of years. The Dogribs fished on the west side [of the North Arm, at *kwenageh*]. There they needed to dig only one hole in the ice to set a net. They tied a rock to a string on the net and rolled the rock down a slope and it carried the net down straight under the ice. When you visited the net you could just pull it out of that hole and then roll it back down again. That's the only place you can do that. Good trout there. The Chipewyans used to camp on the east shore and look for the smoke from the Dogrib campfires and try to get them when they went out to fish.

The Marten Lake people like to get fish there, but they gotta send a smart man who can take fish back from there. Those Chipewyans on the east side by Enotah watch for smoke and run across and kill them. You gotta have good fast men with medicine who can turn themselves into a wolf, fox, wolverine. One man they call *Deneget'a* 'man flies'. He sure runs like he's got wings. He's all alone [an orphan], just his grandma with him. The men go to see about the trout. They can get lots of trout at Lac la Martre, but they gotta show how smart they are to come down here for trout. Flyman was chosen. He runs faster than a fox. He can pass a fox.

They got one dreamer, a prophet. [In another telling of this story, Vital distinguished this "prophet" as a seer—i.e., in Dogrib, 'he knows what's ahead'.] They ask the old man tomorrow what he dream last night. Next morning they go over there. He's still asleep, they wait 'til he wakes up. "Tell us the future," they says. He says, "I don't know why but there is something between Spruce Point and Comb Island. There is something the crow [a carrion eater] is after. It's bad news. One of you should stay behind, especially Flyman. I think you won't reach home." Flyman says, "I got to go, nobody can stop me. Only thing is, my snowshoe strings is worn out. That's all I need." His grandma don't want him to go. She says, "I won't give you strings." He says, "Whatever happens, it's no use to cry. It'll be your own fault."

So they went and they got there and they dig a hole in ice and put in their hooks. In ten, fifteen minutes each got a trout and went into the bush and made a fire to roast their fish. And here come the Chipewyans after them. They start to chase them and they run. Some of them turn into a fox, wolf, or wolverine and take off. Flyman was on his snowshoes. They pass

Old Fort and Flyman's snowshoe string bust. He ties it together and goes on but at Frank's Channel it bust again and he ties it together again. Between Spruce Point and Comb Island it bust again and the enemies caught up to him and killed him. The old man said it would be like that. The last man [of his party] he told, "Tell my old grandma not to cry." That was his last word. He said, she should keep her moosehide forever and never use it, since she was stingy with it when he wanted it.

The Boy Who Changed into a Frog

Like the preceding story, this tale is about a youth endangered by enemies while at a "fishery." But two bits of evidence—the identification of Old Fort Island as the location and the fact that the enemies are not specified as those archvillains, "Akaitcho's bunch"—point to a different era of hostilities. It is not the period (ca. 1812-1830) of Akaitcho and his cohort. Rather it is the 1780s, the time of Cree depredations. The explorer Alexander Mackenzie entered the pertinent facts in his journal on 25 June 1789. Landing on an island "about 5 miles round" he is told by his Chipewyan guide

> that several winters ago . . . this was the land of the Slave Indians [as Dogribs were called in that era] & many of them lived upon the Island round this Bay there being an excellent Fishery all the Year thro' that it was the Crees that drove them away from here by frequently coming to War upon them. If Mr. Leroux [the clerk-trader with Mackenzie] winters in this Country he is to build near this Place on acct. of the Fishery & wood. [McDonald 1966:40]

A boy stayed with his grandmother. They lived at the north end of Marian Lake. All the men of that bunch went to fish at Old Fort Island. He asked his grandmother if he could go, he said he was very hungry. She told him he was too young to go. But he asks again and says he is really hungry for winter trout. She finally says okay but she warns him that not many come home when they fish there. But she gave him a knapsack or something with his blanket and he went. It was his first long trip.

When he got there and the other men too, they put their fishhooks in right away and they got trout right away. So they went to the shore and built a fire and ate good. Before daylight they all went to visit their hooks again and almost everyone got a trout, the boy too. He was cooking his trout and the enemy was coming. The men [with him] turned into different animals, like wolf, fox . . . . The boy was so hungry he just kept eating while the enemy got closer. Just when they got there he turned into a frog and jumped and hid in some spruce boughs. The enemy look all around for him, with their spears they poke around to catch him, but they couldn't catch him. The enemy left when they couldn't find him. After they were gone he turned back into a boy again and checked all the fishhooks of the men and got a big load of trout. He put them in his sack and went back to the camp where his grandmother was. His grandmother is so happy to see him. The men had come back and were sure he was dead because he was still eating when the enemy came. Everyone was sure happy to see him with his big sack of trout.

The Boy with Thunder Medicine

There was a young man with great medicine who wanted to get married. He tells his father and mother, "I think I'll go for a walk so I can find some people." When he says this, his father and mother know he wants to get married. So his father says to him: "I can't stop you. But don't go to the iceberg country. Go into the lowland. Because in the iceberg country the ice is so thick you can't set a net. But inland it is different, the ice is not so thick."

So the young man started out and he had a partner with him. And the first night they make camp. But he thought he was so smart, he says to his partner, "I'm going to the iceberg country to get a wife."

Now, he had great medicine but you got to hide medicine, never mention it. Even now, you can't talk to a man about his medicine. He won't talk about it. If a man talks about it, his medicine gets weak.

So the other fellow said, "That's pretty hard country. I don't want to go, but I'll depend on you. I'll follow you." So they left for the iceberg country. In that country the ice is six or twelve feet thick, it never melts. So in that country if a boy can dig a hole through the ice a man got to give him his daughter because he is so pleased. So they reached a camp in the iceberg country. And the boy went around the camp to find a girl. Some of the girls were showing themselves outside of their tents, trying to make love to him. But in those days a girl that keeps working is a good woman. Finally the boy found a good girl, so he camped there. The next day, before daybreak, he went for a big pile of wood. That's what they did in those days, to please the old man and woman [whose daughter they were courting]. In the old days a boy would never sleep until it was daylight, his parents wouldn't let him.

And the old man, the father of the girl, was telling stories about the ice. "I'm too old, I can't set a net [because the ice is too deep to chop through]. I just bum fish from other people. That's how I live."

Vital Thomas removing fish from net set under the ice. Rae, November 1967.

Now, in that country you got to have the handle on the *edeh* [ice chisel] four fathoms long, because the ice was so thick. But the young man thought it was the same as inland, where you just need a handle one fathom [six feet] long. So the boy cut a handle just one fathom long. And the old woman says, "Poor boy, he doesn't know about the ice here. He is going to have trouble. You better tell him that he needs a long ice handle." But the old man knew, "He must have something in his head. He can do something with a short handle." So the boy makes the handle for the ice chisel and he makes a willow bark net. And *etsin* [the old lady] warned him, "The ice is so thick you can't do much." The boy was cutting a feather from the thunderbird. That is a small bird we have here. Use it for medicine. The boy pick one feather from the thunderbird and tied it to the handle of the ice chisel. And he moves his arm like this [Vital

Bingo (Andrew Ts'etta) using an ice chisel *(edeh).* Rae, 1967.

makes a slow, down-stabbing motion] and soon as the *edeh* touch the ice, it was just like thunder from a rock. With the first [slow, gentle blow] the ice was cracking. And on the second try he hit the ice and yelled, "Here I am hitting you!" And the ice split apart to way out in the ocean. It just opened up [Vital indicates a three- or four-foot crack] and the boy set the net with no trouble, just like it was summertime.

And the whole bunch of iceberg people came running out and they all set their nets. Gee whiz, everybody was happy with that young fellow. They had fish from then right 'til spring.

Medicine men got all different kinds of medicine, some from wolves, some from caribou, bears. This young fellow, he had his spirit from this thunder.

So when the young fellow came back to camp, the old man and woman took a little birch plate, about that big [gestures], and hand it to that girl. And she takes water in it and gives it to the boy to drink. And that means, "We're married."

A man that got spirit from the thunder is a smart man.

Although Gaxieh knew three kinds of wind and Ts'ocia's spirit went with the north pole, this story is the only one that specifically names a phenomenon of nature (thunder) rather than a sentient being as ink'on. *Or is the thunderbird "a small bird we have here," the actual* ink'on? *It seems not.*

Edeh *literally means 'horn'. The aboriginal ice chisel was made of muskox, moose, or caribou horn. After a few blows on the ice, the horn chisel had to be resharpened. As soon as the Dogribs encountered the iron ice chisel in the early fur trade, "All the Indians," in Vital's words, "went crazy for fur" (Helm and Thomas 1966).*

Naidzo told a very different version of the story of the trip to the land of the icebergs—one that did not involve ice fishing or thunder ink'on. *Instead, when the young man announced his intention to travel, his father asked:*

"Do you think you know about *ink'on?*" "Yes." "You know spider?" "Yes." "You know about ants?" "Yes." "You know about shrew?" He said yes to everything. So his dad is pleased. His son can do all *ink'on*. His dad knew his son could go anyplace because his son has enough *ink'on* to stand against anybody.

Yambati

Yambati were around over a thousand years ago. They had fights, they were something like Superman. There were two *yambati*, both Dogribs, and one thinks he's better than the other, kinda jealous. Once while they were out hunting one of them sent a grizzly bear after the other. The other one felt something would happen, but he didn't know what. He was packing a caribou and he kept the string [tumpline] kind of loose so he could just pull the string and the sack would fall off his back. He kept a loose loop so he'd be ready to fight and suddenly a grizzly bear was right in front of him and jumped at him. He pulled the string and let the pack fall and grabbed his club. Those *yambati* always carried clubs to fight, they used bow and arrow just to hunt. As long as he had the club he had power. The bear caught his finger [Vital gestures with his little finger] and broke the bone. But he killed the bear. He went on sick, lame [with his broken finger]. He came back to his camp and found his camp all cleaned [all the people killed] while he was away. He dropped his sack and the other *yambati* went after him. He jumped on a rock at a river bend and hid behind the bank and the other *yambati*'s men came at him with sticks. He grabbed their sticks and killed them. He killed about fifty of them.

The *wedzitxa* [see the account of the qualities of a *wedzitxa*, chap. 5] says [apparently to the surviving followers]: "This is foolish, leave him alone, let him go, this is for two *yambati*. " The crippled one said, "What time do you want to meet me?" The other said, "When the caribou turn gray, when they start to change their hair, watch out for me." The crippled *yambati* had lost all his family, all his men, and he traveled around and his finger was all right again. Then he saw the caribou changing gray for winter and he said, "Now is the time."

He went hunting for the trail of the other *yambati* and he followed the trail. Gee whiz, a big camp. He waited on a hilltop as it came daylight and he saw the *yambati* go to the bush without his men. He cleaned that camp, not a soul alive. Now he waited to fight the *yambati*. I forgot to say that he still had a sister alive. I don't know how she was still alive but they had traveled together. He waited until the *yambati* got home and when that one got home he saw all his men were dead and he threw away his pack and he said, "You killed all my men!" The other said, "A man is a man, he can't stay in one place. What about me? Now you know what it was like for me."

So just those two tried to kill each other with clubs. But they couldn't do it. Their clubs would just meet each other. Then they tried spears too, but the same thing, the spears just hit each other. Then they tried bows and arrows but their arrows just meet each other. So they built fires and try to kill themselves. All their men were dead and they tried to kill themselves fighting. Finally one said, "It's no use, we can't kill each other. We might as well be friends. I have this girl here, you be my brother-in-law until we find some people again." The name of one *yambati* was *Gatco* ('Big Rabbit') and the other was *Etsontih*—caribou guts, like those strings that curve around in the stomach, 'Shits Inside'. *Yambati* means like 'edge of the ocean'.

After the wars stop, no more *yambati. Yambati* would know if enemies were around and he would call out, even if he couldn't see where they are hiding, "You must be there hiding." Then the enemies would just fall down like thunder. Guns won't hurt *yambati*. They fight with clubs.

How the Barrens Came to Be and Went Inside Mountain Got Its Name

On his way to his encounter with the "prophets" at Rae Lakes, the missionary Petitot noted Went Inside Mountain as "a bluff of bare porphyry" with a "bizarre name doubtlessly connected to some absurd tale" (1891:195).

You know that mountain across from *karelin* [a location near the mouth of Marian River]? Indians call that *wedzits'atla* 'Got in the Mountain' or 'Went Inside Mountain'. There is supposed to be somebody in there.

There was a great medicine man. He went hunting and he left his wife behind, alone in the camp. And a young man was out hunting and he find that woman alone. And the young fellow wanted her to go with him. And the woman said, "I'm scared to do that because my husband is a great medicine man. There is no way to hide from him. But I'll go with you anyway."

So the young fellow took the woman with him. When the husband came home there was no woman. And he start to run, try to find out where she went. The young man and the wife headed out toward where the barrens are now. In them days there were no barrens, just bush country. So at last the husband, looking for them, got so mad that he started a fire to burn the bush so he could find them. So they run back. And they get to Marian Lake and climbed up on that mountain. The young man lifted a rock just like you lift a tent. And he told that woman to go inside. So the woman and then the man go inside and he clawed the rock back again.

When the medicine man came he knew they were inside and he was so mad that he started taking rocks out. And he can hear them talking. But he lift one rock here and then he hear them talking someplace else. So he lift a rock there but he hear them someplace else again. Each time he lift a rock they are in some other part of the mountain. Finally, he got tired. He still couldn't reach them. So he said, "So long as the world goes on, you are never coming on the surface of the ground no more." And he left them.

And since then, sometimes medicine guys can hear a noise of those two in the mountain. Not everybody can hear them but some medicine guys can.

And that's also how they made the barrens. Before the medicine man burned the bush, the bush went right through to the Eskimos.

8

Vital Thomas: A Brief Autobiography

Through the years of our friendship I had picked up fragments of Vital's personal history, but usually as conversational asides or imbedded in accounts of some other topic. Eventually I realized that in that form they were almost unrecoverable. In 1970 I asked Vital to recount some of his memories of his earliest years. I had learned in prior years that his mother's native name was Good Paddler. He always spoke of her with a quality of love and respect, often in terms of some wise counsel she had given him.

Earliest Memories

My mother died about 1932 or 1933. She was around sixty when she died. I didn't see my father. I was eight or ten months old when he died. [The band rolls put Vital's birth in 1904.] All my brothers died of TB. It's a good thing they took me out [to mission school at Fort Resolution] before I catch TB. All of my brothers were dead by the time I went to school. I had seven brothers, they all died. And one sister, nine of us altogether. I was the youngest. All my brothers died when young, before they married. One, Michel, was [old enough to be] shooting caribou and ducks. He died when he was about eighteen. In those days, there was no doctor, no hospital, nothing—only the mission.

My mother had a second husband. They called him Fish. She married him while I was at school. They had one child. He died at fifteen or so, TB I think. My mother died before Fish died.

After my father died, my mother lived with her relatives. Her father was Etano, the town [fort] hunter. He was dead before I was born or old enough to know him. I had all kind of uncles around. This was at Trout Rock. My mother had her own tipi. Her relatives were her cousins, so I got to call everyone Uncle. My mother had one sister; she was married

146

to Yathe Nigwi.

My mother set her own nets. Oh, she worked like a man. She sets nets under the ice, and fishhooks. She drives dogs when we move to the caribou. I remember I used to stay in the sleigh [toboggan]. She had a rabbitskin bedroll, I sat on it. When I'd get thirsty and start to cry she'd make a little fire of small sticks and melt snow for water for me to drink. And cold and travel late! And when we find drywood that's the time we put up tipis. But when we are in a rush we make an open camp [without shelter]. And before daylight the men go ahead for hunting. And the women and children drive the dogs and follow the men. Day after day. Only when the men get caribou do we set camp. This would be around December, when we got to get to where the caribou are. We lived at Trout Rock, so we traveled toward the east to the caribou at the edge of the woods. My mother had her own dogs. Her cousins helped with the dog food.

In 1979, during my last visit to Rae, I returned to obtaining from Vital a sustained narrative of his personal history. With a few interpolations and deletions, it is presented in the following passages. Their cadence differs from the prior passages since I talked them from my rough notes into a tape recorder.

Childhood and Youth

In 1912 or 1913 Vital was sent to the Roman Catholic mission school in Resolution. The half dozen children from the Rae area who went were sent to Resolution by York boat. After seven years at Resolution Vital returned on the same York boat. At that time at Rae there was just the mission, the Hudson's Bay Company, and two "free trader" establishments, Lamson Hubbard and Northern Traders (NT).

I went to Resolution school when about six or seven years old. I was at school seven years. I never came home once. When I got back I could hardly speak the language. Soon after I came back to Rae, I got a job from Lamson Hubbard doing the chores around the house. After maybe a year or a little more, NT told me they wanted me to work for them. So I moved to NT and after that Lamson Hubbard asked me to come back. "Because you work good, we will give you a free meal and three dollars a day."

The next year before Christmas they wanted to go to Resolution for freight. They couldn't find nobody to drive the dogs for Jim McDonald [of Northern Traders]. He was crippled so I went to Resolution [as dog driver and McDonald rode in the cariole of the toboggan] with a bunch,

Vital recognized himself and his friend Alexis Crapeau in this photo of the "personnel"
of the mission school at Fort Resolution. Fort Resolution, ca. 1912–17. Duchaussois 1928:
facing p. 289.

eight or nine teams. Some teams were for NT, some for Hudson's Bay,
some were for Lamson Hubbard—they were all sending teams. They
brought an outfit back of what they were short of. After a couple of days
at Resolution we all came back.

To the Barren Ground for Caribou:
A Preview of Treaty (1920–21)

After that, in the fall after freeze-up, Murphy [Monhwi] says, "Everybody
got to go for caribou. No use bumming and staying around the fort." So
everybody went for caribou. There is a lake at the edge of the woods,
Stone Standing Up Lake. All that winter 'til April we stay around that
lake. At the end of April we [and other groups, see below] move back to
the forts.

The Yellowknife bunch [Dogribs from the Yellowknife River], the
Trout Rock bunch, and the people from around here were in that region.
Because Murphy was a big headman the other camps would visit us once
in a while. They would play hands [the hand game] for maybe a day and
then go back to their camp. Maybe in two or three weeks they would
come back and visit Murphy again.

The Yellowknife bunch and the Reliance bunch had one big camp.
They were just out from the Yellowknife River amongst the caribou. They

sent two teams of dogs. They said to Murphy, "We want to have a meeting. In the coming spring they will have Treaty at Rae." So they sent word to Murphy to have a meeting.

About twenty-five teams from Murphy's camp set out. Two friends of my age and I ran ahead of the dogs [on snowshoes] breaking trail. Each of us took turns going first and the other two followed, running behind. When the first man got tired, then another moved up to take his place in the front. That's how we do when the snow is deep. There were about twenty-five teams from Murphy's bunch, and when we get to the Yellowknife and Reliance bunch, their camp, there were about forty families there waiting for Murphy. Lots of people!

They told Murphy, "You are going to get Treaty this spring so we want to have a talk with you. You should say this, say that . . ." Because they [the Yellowknife bunch and the Reliance bunch] had taken Treaty ten years ago. [Actually it was over twenty years. They took Treaty at Fort Resolution, their point of trade, in 1900.] They had taken Treaty ahead of us and we didn't know nothing about Treaty. [Along with other advice] the Yellowknife bunch told Murphy to draw a map [of Dogrib territory], so that is what he done. [Q] I heard the talk between Murphy and the Yellowknife bunch because I stayed in the same tent with Murphy and all of the Yellowknife chiefs and councillors [lesser headmen]. And in the summer [August 1921] we took Treaty. In 1921 Michel Bouvier and Louis Lafferty [two métis] and myself were the only [native] people who could speak English in Fort Rae. [Fumoleau (1975:190–96) presents testimonies of Dogribs, including Vital, who witnessed Treaty.]

The Years with the Police (1922–36)

The same year we took Treaty I was trapping with my step-father and my mother was with us. We stayed across from Old Fort for the winter, we had rabbit snares out and we were fishing, too. That was the first time we ever saw police. We saw one team of dogs coming. We didn't know who it was. "It's not Indians, it's white men!" They came closer and it's the police [Royal Canadian Mounted Police]. That is the first time we see police. About three days before they arrived I had been to Rae to get supplies. When my mother saw the police coming, she said to me, "What have you done? The police don't come for nothing." The police ask me, "You want a job?" They were going to make a cache at Rae Lakes and they offered me the job of running ahead of the dogs at three dollars a day. That was a long run! That was in March. When I told my mother that

Tea dance on Priests' Island, looking toward Hudson's Bay Island, and beyond to Gooseberry Mountain on the mainland. Left to right: NT store, NT office, priests' house, priests' kitchen. In the background, on Hudson's Bay Island, are HBC fish stages, warehouse, interpreter's house, and store. At far right is NT warehouse on Priests' Island. Identifications by Vital Thomas. Fort Rae, 1923. Public Archives of Canada.

the police want me to go with them to Rae Lakes she says, "That's the only way to get a dollar. You'd better go."

So the police came to Fort Rae. [One source says the RCMP post at Rae was officially established in 1924.] Louis Lafferty was the interpreter for the police. But the police needed a guide. So Louis Lafferty was driving one team and Constable Clark was driving one team. The two teams were loaded with grub because the inspector was going to cross from Simpson to Rae. So we took the grub to Rae Lakes. We put up a cache for the inspector but the inspector missed it and they pretty near starved. Finally they found a shack, Old Tatsi's. He had a fish cache but he was gone. The inspector and all of his men stayed there one week and he and his men and dogs used all the fish. When Old Tatsi came into Rae he says, "You pretty near starved our dogs and starved us. You guys stole everything." The police said, "We made a mistake, that's all." They gave Tatsi a hundred dollars for what he lost.

That's the first job I had. The same year, after we came back to Rae, the police asked me to take the place of Louis for interpreter. This was after Easter. I told them, "My grandfather can't hunt much for muskrat [so Vital had to help him]. After the trapping season closes I'll take the job." So that's the way I started with the Mounties [as "special constable"].

I quit twice but they took me back, so finally I stayed fifteen years. [In an earlier account, Vital said it was over eleven years.] In fifteen years I made lots of patrols. In them days there was no game warden, so the police were visiting lots of camps. I've been to Snowdrift, Resolution, Smith, Providence, Hay River. I've been all around this lake patrolling by dogs and by boat.

One time the police and I went to Resolution for mail. We got stuck in Resolution. The inspector from Smith had sent word for us to wait for him. So we waited and spent Christmas there. The inspector came. We left two or three days before New Year's. We spent New Year Day on a low island, the island that is called Nest Island, *et'ondi*. That is the first island from Gros Cap, it's on the open lake. We didn't even have a tent, just an open camp. It was so cold!

Once we went to Fort Smith in March. That was the time when the police barracks at Rae burned. One Mountie, Rod, was burnt badly. He lived twenty-four hours, then he died. Another, Armstrong, his hands and feet were burned. So we took him to Smith to the inspector. That was the time that Sergeant Thorn was here. [Vital continued working for police after the barracks burned. I asked because a couple of whites had intimated to me that Vital was somehow responsible for the fire].

Noemi, Vital Thomas's wife, with Monique Wanazah, a member of the Thomas household. Monique is using a long-bone flesher on the hide of a moose calf. The ethnologist's "shack," as Vital termed it, is in the background. Rae, 1967.

At the time I quit the police I was getting seventy-five dollars a month. When I started with them I got sixty-five dollars a month. After eight or nine years they raised the pay to seventy-five dollars a month. There was no overtime pay. [Q] After I quit the police I never held a full-time job.

The Later Years

In 1936 I moved to Yellowknife with my family. I stayed two years, staking claims. The Yellowknife [gold] mines started in 1934. Then there was just one little shack built in the summer by [Laughlan] Burwash. That was the first mine they found. Burwash had a crew of three guys from Indian Village and me. I worked for him one summer. Indian Village [Dettah] is pretty old, it was there long before Burwash. There were five or six houses in all.

I got married about 1930 [to Noemi, b. 1909]. We had four children. They were dying. We didn't know what TB was like, those days. We had

The foster children of the Thomas household. Left to right: Alfred, Bingo (with snared snowshoe hare), and Babo. Babo is leaning on a bundle of dryfish. Rae, 1967.

to stay up nights with the children, we couldn't get any sleep. I had to quit the job with the police. [Vital and Noemi had at least one child born after the police years. Dora (b. 1945) survived to adulthood. She was struck down by an automobile in Yellowknife at Christmas 1975.]

In the few days remaining in my last visit to Rae, Vital and I did not pick up on the later years in his life. The eventful years of travel were over. Vital and Noemi lived the rest of their life in Rae. Vital kept a dog team but did not take furs except for setting an occasional trap where he or a member of his household sighted "sign" in winter while going to and from fishnets and rabbit snares. I am not aware that in these years he ever hunted big game. He had a shotgun for waterfowl as well as one or two canoes and a kicker (outboard motor). He always kept his equipment in good repair.

By 1967 Noemi was in poor health. Two unmarried women (kin to Noemi, I believe) were part of the household. They carried the woman's work. Tiny Roseanne's specialty was chopping wood. Monique Wanazah was a demon dryfish maker, hide preparer, and just about everything else, including dog team wrangler. Two or three foster children were always part of the household through most of the 1960s and 1970s, each bringing a monthly Canadian "baby bonus" check to the household plus, I believe, some government fosterage payments as well. The household lived comfortably by Rae standards. Vital kept au courant in Dogrib matters

Vital on a pleasure trip to the abandoned site of Old Fort Rae. Between Rae and Old Fort, 1976.

by regular attendance at major social and political events, by frequent contacts with others at the Hudson's Bay store, and through the steady trickle of visitors to the house. Besides working with me intermittently for years (1962–79) as key ethnographic consultant, from 1967 on he worked off and on with several linguists.

Vital Thomas spent the last few years of his life in the Elders' Home in Rae. He died in August 1990 in his eighty-sixth year. In recognition of his years of service to the Royal Canadian Mounted Police, a constable in dress red uniform attended his burial. Linguist Leslie Saxon had visited Vital earlier that summer and found him, though feeble, "still happy to tell stories." It would be good to think that he had succumbed as did the old people of long ago, who, according to Vital, died only when their throats wore through from talking.

Appendix

Dogrib Leadership

In the period treated here, the reservoir from which Dogrib leadership was drawn consisted of men usually aged forty or more who were recognized by their peers as men of sense and probity and who were (or, in the case of very old men, had been) rustlers—good hunters and trappers. For a man to perform a continuing role as a leader, he should also be a "'good talker' . . . who can richly and forcefully express the wisdom based in commitment to and concern with group needs and values" (Helm 1972:81).

After the Dogribs and the other Dene peoples north of Great Slave Lake "signed Treaty" in 1921, the Canadian government required that there be a chief and a set of councillors for the official government "band" of the Rae Dog Ribs. (The Yellowknife B Band had officially come into being in 1900, when leaders of Dogribs trading into Fort Resolution on the south side of Great Slave Lake "signed" Treaty no. 8.) In the Rae Dog Rib Band, to which I will limit discussion, there were in the 1960s seven councillors *(gwatía)* plus the head chief *(gwatindeh)*. The councillors, or "little chiefs," represented a codified and rigidified version of the regional and subregional band leaders of pretreaty times. The Rae Dogribs did not elect a chief and councillors until 1971, two years after the Old Chief retired from office in favor of his son. Until that year they held to the pretreaty tradition of consensual selection of chief and councillors.

The character and performance of leaders and candidates for leadership is always open to assessment and reevaluation by their peers. As one Dogrib explained in respect to councillors:

Just the Indians decide. They [the mature men of the regional group] have a meeting. . . . If a chief is not right they can fire him and get another one to replace him. . . . They talk to each other about that guy who is going to be chief. One of them says [So-and-So should be chief], then another. Four or five guys say he is okay. Then they go tell him they want him to be chief for them. If two or three guys say that one man would be good for chief and others say "no," well, then they just have to choose another.

As his executive arm (his foreman, as Vital puts it) the head chief and each little chief has a *k'awo* selected after discussion between the chief and the consequential men of his group. The term *k'awo*—'he who says *"k'a!"* [wait!]',—can be applied to any kind of boss or organizer, including the head chief. Certain activities undertaken by a set of persons, such as the men's fall caribou hunt or the moving of an advance camp, require *k'awos* selected for the duration of the enterprise. It was as such a task-group *k'awo* that a younger man might occasionally be chosen. "He's young but he's steady," was the judgment on a thirty-four-year-old man being considered for *k'awo* of a caribou-hunt crew.

As a polity, for a hundred years the Dogribs trading into Fort Rae had, through three long-lived men, a kind of paramount leadership unique among the Dene peoples of the Mackenzie region. It began with the Old Chief's father and ended when the Old Chief stepped down at treaty time in 1969. The Old Chief at the age of fifty-two came to office in 1934 as the designate of the dying chief Monhwi (Murphy), who had signed Treaty in 1921. The latter had been the designate in 1902 of the Old Chief's father, the great trading chief Ekawi Dzimi, who had been a prime leader for thirty-five years. (For a fuller exposition of leader statuses and roles and changing terminology through time, see Helm 1965, 1972:77–78, and 1979:151–52.)

The role of the Old Chief as "the flag" of the Dogrib people ended only with his death in January 1975 at ninety-three or ninety-four years of age:

The old man [the Chief] is pretty sick right now . . . last month all the Lac la Martre [Marten Lake] old people chartered a plane to come see him . . . to shake hands. And a whole bus load of old people came from the village at Yellowknife [Dettah] came to shake hands with the old man. [Letter from Vital Thomas dated 6 December 1974. All letters from him are written for him at his dictation.]

The old man . . . died on the 16th of January. The Indians came from Lac la Martre, Rae Lakes, Snare Lake, Yellowknife in chartered planes. It cost around $2012 for that. Everyone chipped in some money. The bishop [of the Northwest Territories] and a priest from Smith and from Yellowknife came to the funeral. This has never happened before. [Letter from Vital dated 25 January 1975.]

A young Dogrib woman later described the Old Chief's funeral: His coffin rested in the church for three days and the people of Rae had feasts for two nights in memory of him. They waited to bury him to give him special honor in the church, to wait for people from other communities to arrive, and to hope for warmer weather for the burial. Many people did come and over $1000 was collected. Whites sent fresh flowers [from Yellowknife] to the service and two Mounties in full dress attended the coffin throughout the service. Some people wanted the Old Chief to go to the hospital about a week before he died, but he said no. He wanted to die at home and the time had come. He died quietly in his sleep, he was in no pain, and the people were happy he died so peacefully.

Notes

Chapter 1. Prelude to Prophecy

1. At that time, 1914, when these Dogribs disassociated themselves from Rae as their point of trade, they switched their trade to Fort Norman for Fort Franklin was at that time closed as a trading post. The ethnic histories and interactions of the Dene peoples trading into Forts Norman and Franklin are complex. See Gillespie (1981) on the "Bearlake Indians" and Osgood (1932:32–35) on the "Satudene."

2. See Moore and Wheelock (1990:94–100) for specific identifications of the regional groups involved who may be included under the rubrics *Slavey* and/or *Beaver*. Here I use the names of settlements or locales used by Dogribs to identify places where the Slavey prophets were to be found. Moore and Wheelock make more precise identifications of persons and locales.

3. The Rae Dogribs returned with the news that two other persons had "started preaching at Bear Lake." One was a woman, a granddaughter of the late Dogrib prophet Ayha (see below), whom they recorded on cassette tape.

4. "*'Nahwit'in* 'I dream'. When you say this, then people know that *ink'on* has talked to you," according to Vital.

5. The word Chi used was *enitl'e*. It can refer to a piece of paper or a picture. While translating from the tape, Vital said "picture." Upon consideration, however, he concluded, "I think he means a sign with writing on paper, because when we used to travel through the bush if you find a sign with writing on it we would yell *'enitl'e da woci'*. There must have been writing on it; he talked about reading it." The Catholic Oblate missionaries to the Dene adapted a syllabary developed for the Cree to the Athapaskan languages of Chipewyan and Dogrib. The Dogrib syllabary was available at Rae in 1912 for "study" by Wheeler (1914:48,

51–52), who provides a copy in his report. Russell (1898:99) describes "Yellow Knife" chiefs (Chipewyans in Vital's classification) at Resolution in the early 1890s wanting "pencils and paper for writing letters in syllabics when sending for supplies." On the other hand, see the question of the "Catholic ladder" as the model. The ladder presents scenes with both figures and words.

6. *Sacrifice,* as used by Vital, apparently refers to controlling oneself in order to do good or be good.

7. A reference to the drums with ribbons used by the Alberta prophets and by Jack and the Rae minor prophets.

Chapter 2. Message, Performance, and Persona

1. In 1976 a plebiscite at Rae resulted in the prohibition of possession or consumption of alcohol within thirty miles of the settlement. Outlying Dogrib bush hamlets followed suit, as did a number of other settlements in the Northwest Territories populated mainly by Dene peoples. In a subsequent year Rae voted to go "wet," but in the fall of 1986 a plebiscite again approved prohibition by a narrow margin *(News/North,* 6 February 1987). Whatever damping effect community proscriptions may have had on alcohol consumption, alcohol abuse remains a serious problem among the Dene and Inuit (Eskimo) of the Northwest Territories.

2. Since I attended the prophet dance ceremony in the face of my knowledge of Jack's concerns about whites, this is an appropriate point to say something about my style of inquiry and deportment in the field in general and my presence at the prophet ceremony in particular. I do not knowingly pressure or cause distress or embarrassment to members of a host population. If I sense that an individual does not want to answer a question or feels uneasy about a topic, I drop it. If I grasp that my presence in his or her dwelling in causing a person discomfort, I soon depart. Unless I am remarkably obtuse about these matters, I have only a few times met with such reactions from Dene. I grant that Dene "shyness" (except when drunk) to reveal a negative reaction to another person may have on occasion misled me as to an individual's feelings.

Given Vital's antipathy to Jack's prophecy, I made no effort to ask him to seek out Jack or one of the minor prophets for discussion or interview. Nor could I hurt Vital by seeking another person to serve as interpreter and conduit to Jack or his adherents. I might have worked this problem through had not my fieldtrips been so brief.

On the day of the big ceremony at the prophet corral, Vital was in Dettah (and trying that evening to promote a ride back for "the dance"). As I stood with some Dogribs watching the first canoes depart for the prophet dance I commented to a middle-aged male acquaintance, "I'd sure like to go along, but I wonder if the people would want a stranger." He promptly assured me, "Anybody can go." Then one of Jack's elderly adherents, with whom I had a lighthearted relationship, spotted me as his boat was pulling out and made dancing movements with his body, signaling, "Come on!" When I discovered that the household of another friend was making preparations to go I asked if I could accompany them. "Sure." At the prophet dance I kept a low profile. In the course of the evening Barthelemy and a minor-prophet acquaintance and I exchanged handshakes, smiles, and few words. One woman, a young mother I had known as a helpful teenager at Marten Lake, seemed not to want to interact with me at the prophet dance, although our friendship thereafter remained as before. On two occasions that evening male friends came up and initiated a conversation in English. Though I responded only in low monosyllables, the English provoked disapproving glances from some middle-aged women standing nearby. Outside the prophet corral, I shook hands with the Prophet's wife but did not approach Jack, nor he me.

In sum, I decided to take the view demonstrated to me by others that "the dance" was not Jack's proprietary but a public event open to everyone.

3. A brief description by Goulet (1982:11–12) of a prophet dance held by the Alberta Dene confirms several points of correspondence with the Dogrib ceremony: a corral with tall poles flying emblematic flags; offerings (tobacco only) with genuflections and signings of the cross to accompaniment of drumming-singing by prophets; the burning of the offerings in the fire in the center of the corral. Moore and Wheelock (1990:61) provide essentially the same description. Ridington's (1978:25) account of Beaver prophet dance performances, presumably of the 1960s, specifies only a central fire in "usually a large temporary dance lodge"; apparently, there were no flags, burnt offerings, signing of the cross, genuflecting, nor other Christian expressions of any kind. In fact, Ridington's monograph on the Beaver prophet dance (1978) gives no indication that the Beaver Indians of the upper Peace River had any knowledge of Christianity in the 1960s (and were in fact communicants in the Roman Catholic Church) except the statement that "Jesus and Saya became co-existent-culture heroes" (1978:49). Moore and Wheelock do not address the Catholic ties of the Alberta prophets.

4. According to Naidzo, the issue was that the fur trader at Rae refused

to give the chief and his men, including Naidzo, who had come in to trade, the customary matches, tobacco, and food for a feast before trading commenced. Osgood, perhaps reporting a statement by his interpreter and informant at Fort Norman (A. W. Boland), says that the Bear Lake Dogribs "left Rae in 1914 as a result of an epidemic of sickness there" (1932:73).

5. Although the Rae community hall, a government building, was built for the use of the Dogrib populace, the mountie was refusing to release the keys to Jack because the hall had been left in a mess after its last use. So Lurie and I were brought into action as whites to extract the keys from the mountie.

6. In reviewing the tapes of the treaty feast I asked: How did the people react to Jack's announcement that he would not join the feast?

Vital: "No one said Jack was right. If they had thought he was right they would have said *ekwia di* 'It's the truth', but nobody said that."

7. The school, opened in 1971, was built at Edzo, a new town site a few miles from Rae. The government's plan was to relocate all Dogrib residents of Rae to Edzo, but the Rae Dogribs simply refused to be moved. The children were bused to school daily.

Chapter 3. The Foundations of Prophecy

1. Unlike Old Testament prophets, Naidzo specified he did not see God, let alone enter into a dialogue with him. It was said, however, that Jack said *he* had seen God.

2. It seems that the 1960s saw the start of self-conscious examination of their ministry among the Dene by the Oblates in the Northwest Territories, as individuals and as a network. René Fumoleau, O.M.I., provides insightful personal testimony. He was resident priest in Fort Franklin in 1968 when "the prophetic movement" reached that settlement (i.e., when Jack the Rae Prophet and his retinue of Dogribs arrived by dog team):

> I didn't have the proper mental categories to analyze this movement. I had also been ill-advised about it, and I didn't know how to react to this cultural and religious movement. However, I could feel that my "traditional" ministry among the Dene had come to an end. The renewed self-awareness among the Dene was incompatible with a priestly ministry based on western culture and more or less equated with the

"sacred" things. [1982:143]

3. To Sam Stanley "the Northwest Territories people . . . seemed to be the most unsophisticated of all the groups who came [to Morley]. I think part of this was because they could not readily trot out pipe, sweet grass, tobacco, and all the other accoutrements which were so widespread in the States and southern Canada. The other part has to do with their relative isolation from, until recently, all other Native peoples in North America. No pan-Indian movements, BIA boarding schools, Pow-wows, etc." (p. c.).

4. Petitot (1865) identifies the group he visited as *Takwel-Ottiné*. The range of this group conforms to that of *et'at'in*.

5. In his later account Petitot (1891:223) says five, one a woman.

6. Elsewhere, Petitot (1893:98–101) described a Slavey, a "crazy man" at Fort Norman, whose visions led him to believe himself a "priest" of God, and an aged Dene at Fort Good Hope who presented himself as the "Eternal Father," confessing, baptizing, and singing mass until his wife announced her "vision from God" that her husband was a liar, while she was the "Holy Virgin" (Petitot 1879:7–8).

7. A news item in the *1989 Dene Nation Annual Report* reveals that at Fort Franklin "the grand opening of the Prophet Ayha's House was held in August 1989, with the help of the Lac La Martre people who helped the house with materials and transportation provided by the Fort Franklin band."

8. Janes and Kelley (1977) have surveyed the nineteenth and twentieth century literature in English for evidence of "crisis cult activities" among the Dene of the Mackenzie Basin. Some of the preternatural-inspired actors are referred to as prophets in the sources. This is a useful compilation, but the assumption of "crisis" causation raises as many evidential questions as it purports to answer.

9. These groups—reported in Goddard (1916), Ridington (1978), Goulet (1989), and Moore and Wheelock (1990)—share prophet dance understandings and activities with neighboring Crees. The westerly Beaver abut the "Western Dene," who formed the northern extension of tribes manifesting the Northwest Prophet Dance of the nineteenth century, as analyzed by Spier (1935).

10. The statement of Moore and Wheelock (1990:xxii) that "all Dene Dhaa [the Hay Lakes Dene] songs are prayers" certainly does not hold for Dogrib tea dance songs; witness such lyrics as "[You] men on the rock, good dance, hurry-up!" and "Baptiste's mother, make tea!" (Helm and Lurie 1966:18; Helm and Thomas 1966:53–54).

11.   The manifestation of satanic forces was a live question for the

early missionaries to the Indians of eastern Canada. The Jesuit Brebeuf, for example, reporting in his *Relations* (of 1634-36) on the performances of the curing society of the Hurons, concluded that "in my opinion, these people are true sorcerers who have access to the devil" (Talbot 1956:72). Some 240 years later, Petitot (1876:224) defined the Dene "*jongleur ou chaman*" as only "*prétendu magicien sauvage.*"

12. See Ridington (1988) for an analytic review of the contributions of ethnographers, including Goulet, to understandings of the "native thought world" of the Subarctic Algonkian and Athapaskan peoples.

13. Grim's (1983:180-85) discussion of the shaman and prophet as religious types is apposite here.

References

Basso, Ellen B.
    1978   The Enemy of Every Tribe: "Bushman" Images in Northern Athapaskan Narratives. American Ethnologist 5(4): 690–709.

Berger, Thomas R.
    1977   Northern Frontier, Northern Homeland: The Report of the Mackenzie Valley Pipeline Inquiry. 2 vols. Ottawa: Minister of Supply and Services, Canada.

Boas, Franz
    1910   Religion. *In* Handbook of American Indians North of Mexico, edited by Frederick Webb Hodge. Smithsonian Institution, Bureau of American Ethnology, Bulletin no. 30, vol. 2, 365–71. Washington, D.C.: Government Printing Office.

Brightman, Robert
    1988   The Windigo in the Material World. Ethnohistory 35(4): 337–79.

Canada
    1970   Linguistic and Cultural Affiliations of Canadian Indian Bands. Department of Indian Affairs and Northern Development. Ottawa: Queen's Printer.

Duchaussois, Pierre
    1928   Aux glaces polaires: Indiens et Esquimaux. Nouvelle edition. Paris: Editions SPES.

Fumoleau, Réné
    1975   As Long as This Land Shall Last. Toronto: McClelland and Stewart.

    1982   Missionary among the Dene. Kerygma no. 37: 139–66. Ottawa.

Gillespie, Beryl C.
    1981   Bearlake Indians. *In* Subarctic, edited by June Helm. Handbook of North American Indians, vol. 6:310–13. Washington, D.C.: Smithsonian Institution.

Goddard, Pliny E.
    1916   Beaver Indians. Anthropological Papers of the American Museum of Natural History, vol. 10, part 4.

Goulet, Jean-Guy
    1982   Religious Dualism among Athapaskan Catholics. Canadian Journal of Anthropology 3(1): 1–18.

1989   Representation of Self and Reincarnation among the Dene-tha.
            Culture 8(2): 3–18.
1990   Ways of Knowing with the Mind: An Ethnology of Aboriginal
            Beliefs. Ms.
Grim, John A.
1983   The Shaman. Norman: University of Oklahoma Press.
Handelman, Don
1968   Shamanizing on an Empty Stomach. American Anthropologist
            70:353–56.
Hanley, Philip M.
1973   Father Lacombe's Ladder. Etudes Oblates (April-June): 82–99.
            Ottawa.
Helm, June
1961   The Lynx Point People: The Dynamics of a Northern
            Athapaskan Band. National Museum of Canada Bulletin no.
            176. Ottawa.
1965   Patterns of Allocation among the Arctic Drainage Dene. *In*
            Essays in Economic Anthropology, edited by June Helm, Paul
            Bohannan, and Marshall D. Sahlins, 33–45. Proceedings of the
            1965 Annual Spring Meeting of the American Ethnological
            Society. Seattle: University of Washington Press.
1972   The Dogrib Indians. *In* Hunters and Gatherers Today: A
            Socioeconomic Study of Eleven Such Cultures in the Twentieth
            Century, edited by M. G. Bicchieri, 51–89. New York: Holt,
            Rinehart and Winston.
1979   Long-Term Research among the Dogrib and Other Dene. *In*
            Long-Term Field Research in Social Anthropology, edited by
            G. M. Foster, Thayer Scudder, Elizabeth Colson, and Robert
            Van Kemper, 145–63. New York: Academic Press.
1980   Indian Dependency and Indian Self-Determination: Problems
            and Paradoxes in Canada's Northwest Territories. *In* Political
            Organization of Native North Americans, edited by Ernest L.
            Schusky, 215–42. Washington, D.C.: University Press of
            America.
1981a   Dogrib. *In* Subarctic, edited by June Helm. Handbook of North
            American Indians, vol. 6:291–309. Washington, D.C.:
            Smithsonian Institution.
1981b   Dogrib Folk History and the Photographs of John Alden Mason:
            Indian Occupation and Status in the Fur Trade, 1900–1925.
            Arctic Anthropology 18(2): 43–58.
Helm, June, George A. DeVos, and Teresa Carterette
1963   Variations in Personality and Ego Identification within a Slave
            Indian Kin-Community. National Museum of Canada Bulletin
            no. 190:94–138.
Helm, June, and Beryl C. Gillespie
1981   Dogrib Oral Tradition as History: War and Peace in the 1820s.
            Journal of Anthropological Research 37(1): 8–27.
Helm, June, and Nancy O. Lurie
1966   The Dogrib Hand Game. National Museum of Canada Bulletin

no. 205. Ottawa.

Helm, June, Edward W. Rogers, and James G. E. Smith
1981   Intercultural Relations and Cultural Change in the Shield and
            Mackenzie Borderlands. *In* Subarctic, edited by June Helm.
            Handbook of North American Indians, vol. 6:146-57.
            Washington, D.C.: Smithsonian Institution.

Helm, June, and Vital Thomas
1966   Tales from the Dogribs. The Beaver, Outfit 297 (autumn):
            16-20; Outfit 297 (winter): 52-54.

Honigmann, John J.
1975   Psychological Traits in Northern Athapaskan Culture. *In*
            Proceedings: Northern Athapaskan Conference, 1971, edited by
            A. M. Clark. National Museum of Man, Mercury Series,
            Canadian Ethnology Service Paper 27(2): 545-76.

Janes, Robert R., and Jane H. Kelley
1977   Observations on Crisis Cult Activities in the Mackenzie Basin.
            In Problems in the Prehistory of the North American Subarctic:
            The Athapaskan Question, edited by J. W. Helmer, S. Van
            Dyke, and F. J. Kense, 153-64. Calgary: Archeological
            Association, University of Calgary.

Jenness, Diamond
1922   The Life of the Copper Eskimos. Report of the Canadian Arctic
            Expedition 1913-18, Vol. 12. Ottawa: F. A. Acland, Printer to
            the King's Most Excellent Majesty.

McDonald, T. H., ed.
1966   Exploring the Northwest Territory: Sir Alexander Mackenzie's
            Journal. Norman: University of Oklahoma Press.

MacNeish, June Helm
1954   Contemporary Folk Beliefs of a Slave Indian Band. Journal of
            American Folklore 67(264): 185-98.

McPhail, J. D., and C. C. Lindsey
1970   Freshwater Fishes of Northwestern Canada and Alaska.
            Fisheries Research Board of Canada Bulletin no. 173. Ottawa.

Mason, John Alden
1946   Notes on the Indians of the Great Slave Lake. Yale University
            Publications in Anthropology no. 34.

Merriam-Webster
1940   New International Dictionary of the English Language. Second
            edition. Springfield, Mass.: G. & C. Merriam.

Mooney, James
1896   The Ghost-Dance Religion and the Sioux Outbreak of 1890.
            Smithsonian Institution, Bureau of Ethnology, 14th Annual
            Report. Washington, D.C.: Government Printing Office.

Moore, Patrick, and Angela Wheelock, eds.
1990   Wolverine Myths and Visions: Dene Traditions from Northern
            Alberta. Lincoln: University of Nebraska Press.

Morice, A. G.
1971   The History of the Northern Interior of British Columbia. 1905.
            Reprint, Fairfield, Wash.: Ye Galleon Press.

Müller, Werner
1989   The Far North. *In* Native American Religions: North America,
          edited by Lawrence E. Sullivan, 99-110. New York:
          Macmillan.
Nabokov, Peter, ed.
1991   Native American Testimony. New York: Viking.
News/North
1987   Liquor Seized Despite Prohibition. *In* News/North 6 February
          1987. Yellowknife, NWT.
Osgood, Cornelius
1932   The Ethnography of the Great Bear Lake Indians. National
          Museum of Canada Bulletin no.70:31-97. Ottawa.
Petitot, Emile
1865   Letter from Mission de St. Michel, Fort Rae, 22 June 1864.
          Annales de la Propagation de la Foi 37 (1865): 377-93.
1876   Dictionnaire de la langue Déné-Dindjié. Paris: E. Leroux.
1888   Traditions indiennes du Canada nord-west: Textes originaux et
          traduction littérale. Alençon: E. Renaut-de Broise.
1891   Autour du Grand Lac des Esclaves. Paris: A. Savine.
1893   Exploration de la region du Grand Lac des Ours. Paris: Tequi.
Ridington, Robin
1978   Swan People: A Study of the Dunne-za Prophet Dance.
          National Museum of Man Mercury Series, Canadian Ethnology
          Service Paper 38.
1981   Beaver. *In* Subarctic, edited by June Helm. Handbook of North
          American Indians, vol. 6:350-60. Washington, D.C.:
          Smithsonian Institution.
1988   Knowledge, Power, and the Individual in Subarctic Hunting
          Societies. American Anthropologist 90(1): 98-110.
Roberts, John M.
1964   The Self-Management of Cultures. *In* Explorations in Cultural
          Anthropology, edited by Ward H. Goodenough, 433-54. New
          York: McGraw-Hill.
Rushforth, Scott
1981   Speaking to "Relatives-Through-Marriage": Aspects of
          Communication among the Bear Lake Athapaskans. Journal of
          Anthropological Research 37(1): 28-45.
1992   The Legitimation of Belief in a Hunting-Gathering Society:
          Bearlake Athapaskan Knowledge and Authority. American
          Ethnologist 19(3): 483-500.
Russell, Frank
1898   Explorations in the Far North: Being the Report of an
          Expedition under the Auspices of the University of Iowa during
          the Years 1892, 1893, and 1894. Iowa City: University of Iowa.
Scollon, Ron, and Suzanne B. K. Scollon
1984   Cooking It Up and Boiling It Down: Abstracts in Athabaskan
          Children's Story Retellings. *In* Coherence in Spoken and
          Written Discourse, edited by Deborah Tannen. Advances in
          Discourse Processes 12:173-97. Norwood, N.J.: ABLEX

Publishing Corporation.

Slobodin, Richard
    1981   Subarctic Métis. *In* Subarctic, edited by June Helm. Handbook
                of North American Indians, vol. 6:361–71. Washington, D.C.:
                Smithsonian Institution.

Smith, David M.
    1973   Inkonze: Magico-Religious Beliefs of Contact-Traditional
                Chipewyan Trading at Fort Resolution, NWT, Canada. National
                Museum of Man, Mercury Series, Ethnology Division Paper no.
                6.
    1988   The Concept of Medicine-Power in Chipewyan Thought. Ms.
    1990   The Chipewyan Medicine Fight in Cultural and Ecological
                Perspective. *In* Culture and the Anthropological Tradition:
                Essays in Honor of Robert F. Spencer, edited by Robert H.
                Winthrop, 153–75. Lanham, Md.: University Press of America.

Smith, James G. E.
    1978   The Emergence of the Micro-Urban Village among the
                Caribou-Eater Chipewyan. Human Organization 37(1): 38–49.

Spier, Leslie
    1935   The Prophet Dance of the Northwest and Its Derivatives: The
                Source of the Ghost Dance. American Anthropological
                Association General Series in Anthropology 1. Menasha,
                Wisconsin.

Spiro, Melford E.
    1966   Religion: Problems of Definition and Explanation. *In*
                Anthropological Approaches to the Study of Religion, edited
                by Michael Banton, 85–126. London: Tavistock Publications.

Stanley, Sam
    1977   American Indian Power and Powerlessness. *In* The Anthro-
                pology of Power, edited by Raymond D. Fogelson and Richard
                N. Adams, 237–42. New York: Academic Press.

Talbot, Francis Xavier
    1956   Saint among the Hurons: The Life of Jean de Brebeuf. Garden
                City, N.J.: Image Books, Doubleday.

Wallace, Anthony F. C.
    1966   Religion: An Anthropological View. New York: Random
                House.

Wheeler, David E.
    1914   The Dog-Rib Indian and His Home. Bulletin of the Geo-
                graphical Society of Philadelphia 12(2): 47–69.

Personal Name Index

Abel, Susie (Joseph), xii
Akaitcho, 33, 78, 131–35, 138
Alberta Prophet, 14, 35, 37; rituals of, 71; teachings of, 28, 48, 56; visited by Jack, 18; visits by, 14–15, 18–19, 27, 30–31, 47
Alfred, 153 (photo)
Alphonse W, 109
Amourous, Jean, O.M.I., 125–26
Armstrong, R.C.M.P., 151
Arrowmaker, Alexis, 89
Ayah. *See* Ayha
Ayha, 65, 158

Babo, 153 (photo)
Barthelemy (pseudonym), 19, 25, 40, 57, 160; as band councillor, 12, 52; birth date, 12; invites Alberta Prophet, 14; son of, 54; speech by, 49; visited by Chi, 31
Base, Johnny, xii
Bear Lake Chief, 46, 106, 123–24
Bearlake, Harry, xii, 93 (photo)
Bearlake, Toby, 96–97
Beaulieu, Elise, xii
Beaulieu, Jeremy, 127
Beaulieu, John, 125, 127
Beaulieu, Philip, 83
Beaverhook, 120, 127

Beaverhook's widow, 119 (photo), 120
Big Boiling Mouth, 8 (photo legend)
Bighead, John, 95–96
Bingo, xii, 83, 141 (photo), 153 (photo)
Boas, Franz, 77
Boniface, 98–100
Boss for the Nets. *See* Tamin K'awo
Bouvier, Michel, 149
Brebeuf, Jean de, S.J., 163
Bruneau, Jimmie, xii
Bruneau, Susie (Joseph), xii
Burwash, Laughlan, 152

Casimir, 85
Charlo, Alexis, xii
Chi (pseudonym), 2, 48, 67; and *ink'on,* 20, 68; and *tsinco,* 20, 127, 129; as prophet, 13, 18–22, 25, 30, 34, 47, 53, 58, 71; birth date, 12; persona, 41–42, 45–46, 54, 60, 71; rituals of, 59; teachings of, 27–29; travels of, 14–15, 31, 43, 56; visions of, 44–45, 56, 59–60, 158; visited by Helm, 43